W.

WINNING BASKETBALL PLAYS

BY AMERICA'S FOREMOST COACHES

Edited by
CLAIR BEE

A · S · BARNES and COMPANY
New York

Published on the same day in the Dominion of Canada
by The Copp Clark Co., Limited, Toronto

This book is dedicated to NED IRISH, vice-president of Madison Square Garden, for his many invaluable contributions to basketball as executive, amicable critic and steadfast friend.

Basketball owes much of its present tremendous national popularity to Ned. His intersectional collegiate doubleheaders, first presented in the Garden in 1934, lifted the game from a relatively obscure spot among America's sports to a position unrivaled by any other athletic activity.

Clair Bee

ACKNOWLEDGMENTS

The editor wishes particularly to acknowledge the contributions made to this book by the following coaches: Forrest C. (Phog) Allen, University of Kansas; Justin (Sam) Barry, University of Southern California; John Bunn, Springfield College; Howard (Jake) Cann, New York University; Harold C. (Red) Carlson, University of Pittsburgh; Everett Case, North Carolina State University; Forrest (Frosty) Cox, University of Colorado; Everett Dean, Stanford University; Bruce Drake, University of Oklahoma; Harold E. (Bud) Foster, University of Wisconsin; Amory T. (Slats) Gill, Oregon State College; Jack Gray, University of Texas; Lawrence (Pops) Harrison, the State University of Iowa; Edgar S. Hickey, St. Louis University; Paul D. (Tony) Hinkle, Butler University; Howard Hobson, Yale University; Nat Holman, College of the City of New York; Henry P. Iba, Oklahoma Agricultural and Mechanical College; Alvin (Doggie) Julian, Boston Celtics; Edward (Moose) Krause, University of Notre Dame; Joseph Lapchick, New York Knickerbockers; Arthur C. (Dutch) Lonborg, Northwestern University; Branch (Big Mac) McCracken, University of Indiana; Vadal Peterson, University of Utah; Herbert W. (Buck) Read, Western Michigan College; Adolph F. Rupp, University of Kentucky; Wilbur (Sparky) Stalcup, University of Missouri.

In addition the editor wishes to thank the following coaches for their contributions of individual scoring plays: Lewis P. Andreas, Syracuse University; Forrest Anderson, Bradley University; E. Al Baggett, Brooklyn College; Buster Brannon, Texas Christian University; Ben L. Carnevale, U. S. Naval Academy; Harry Combes, University of Illinois; George P. Dahlberg, Montana State University; Al Duer, George Pepperdine College; William (Tippy) Dye, Ohio State University; Loren Ellis, Calumet Buccaneers; Fred A. Enke, University of Arizona; Jack Friel, Washington State College; John (Taps) Gallagher, Niagara University; Jack H. Gardner, Kansas State College; Kenneth C. Gerard, Duke University; Henry C. Good, University of Nebraska; Blair Gullion, Washington University; Tom Haggerty, University of Loyola; R. E. (Bill) Henderson, Baylor University; Marty Karow, Texas A. & M. College; Frank Keaney, Rhode Island State College; Eugene Lambert, University of Arkansas; Elmer A. Lampe, Dartmouth College; Glen (Jake) Lawlor, University of Nevada; John Lawther, Penn State College; Kenneth Loeffler, La Salle College; Emmett Lowery, University of Tennessee; John W. Mauer, U. S.

Military Academy; Albert McClellan, Boston College; Frank McGuire, St. John's University; Art McLarney, University of Washington; Donald (Dudey) Moore, Duquesne University; Benjamin H. Neff, St. Mary's College; Peter F. Newell, University of San Francisco; Joseph P. Niland, Canisius College; Kenneth (Red) Norton, Manhattan College; Ray S. Pesca, University of Santa Clara; C. M. (Nibs) Price, University of California; Gordon Ridings, Columbia University; Elmer H. Ripley, John Carroll University; Tom Scott, University of North Carolina; Everet F. Shelton, University of Wyoming; Gus K. Tebell, University of Virginia; W. J. Trautwein, Ohio University; John Warren, University of Oregon; Clifford Wells, Tulane University; Donald S. White, Rutgers University; John Wiethe, University of Cincinnati.

CONTENTS

BASKETBALL COACHES' CREED
by
George R. Edwards
University of Missouri

I BELIEVE that basketball has an important place in the general educational scheme and pledge myself to cooperate with others in the field of education to so administer it that its value never will be questioned.

I BELIEVE that others of this sport are as earnest in its protection as I am, and I will do all in my power to further their endeavors.

I BELIEVE that my own actions should be so regulated at all times that I will be a credit to the profession.

I BELIEVE that the members of the National Basketball Committee are capably expressing the rules of the game, and I will abide by these rules in both spirit and letter.

I BELIEVE in the exercise of all the patience, tolerance, and diplomacy at my command in my relations with all players, co-workers, game officials and spectators.

I BELIEVE that the proper administration of this sort offers an effective laboratory method to develop in its adherents high ideals of sportsmanship; qualities of cooperation, courage, unselfishness and self-control; desires for clean, healthful living; and respect for wise discipline and authority.

I BELIEVE that these admirable characteristics, properly instilled by me through teaching and demonstration, will have a long carry-over and will aid each one connected with the sport to become a better citizen.

I BELIEVE in and will support all reasonable moves to improve athletic conditions, to provide for adequate equipment and to promote the welfare of an increased number of participants.

A WORD TO THE BEGINNING COACH

I hope the conclusions which the beginning coach may draw from a study and analysis of the formations and plays presented in this book will aid him in selecting a formation or formations and style of play which will be best suited to the personnel he has available. However, before he makes a decision, a brief discussion of the principles underlying basketball offenses may be in order.

Presumably, a coach should choose a certain basketball formation and its accompanying plays because it utilizes most effectively the offensive skills of the players he has available. However, this is seldom true. In a great many cases a coach employs a formation and certain plays because he was *schooled* in that style as a player. Again, coaches sometimes *adopt* a style of play because it is effectively used by some renowned coach or because it was used in winning a championship. Not infrequently a coach *inherits* a style of play because, in a new position, he finds a veteran team thoroughly drilled in a certain formation and its plays and he is reluctant to risk a change.

An increasing number of coaches prefer to choose a permanent style of play. Therefore, incoming players are trained for the various positions by means of an apprentice or understudy system. This is a specialized method and goes hand in hand with control basketball.

Whatever the reason for the selection of a particular attack, two important principles are present and worthy of consideration. These principles will be presented in question and answer form.

WHAT IS MEANT BY MAN-AHEAD-OF-THE-BALL?

Man-ahead-of-the-ball means that an attempt is made to free a player so that he may advance toward the basket ahead of the ball. When he has eluded his opponent through personal efforts (footwork, change of pace, change of direction, speed, etc.) or because of screens and blocks by his teammates, the ball is passed forward to him so that he may attempt a score.

WHAT IS MEANT BY BALL-AHEAD-OF-THE-MAN?

Ball-ahead-of-the-man means that one or more players will be stationed near the basket and the ball will be passed to one of these players before or simultaneously with the development of the play. Thereafter, cutting and/or screening principles are employed to free a teammate who can cut toward the ball, receive a pass, and try for a score.

WHY ARE THESE TWO PRINCIPLES IMPORTANT IN CONSIDERING THE VARIOUS ATTACKING FORMATIONS?

These two principles are important because they determine the effectiveness of formation positions. Man-ahead-of-the-ball requires that the area in front of and near the basket (between the ball and the cutting player) be kept open.

This means that the formation must position the majority of its players in the rear of the frontcourt or near the sidelines if they are placed near the baseline.

Ball-ahead-of-the-man requires one or more pivot or post players stationed in the vicinity of the free-throw line or closer to the basket with the express purpose of handling the ball and feeding it to cutting teammates who drive forward from the rear of the frontcourt. (These pivot and post players are expected to score themselves.)

In the ball-ahead-of-the-man style of play, the post or pivot men must not be stationed too close together, or to the basket, because of the danger of congesting the basket area and limiting the ability of teammates to maneuver after receiving the ball.

WHAT STYLES EMPLOY BALL-AHEAD-OF-THE-MAN?

All formations which use the single post, double post, pivot, double pivot, or combinations of post and pivot.

WHAT ARE THE NAMES GIVEN TO MAN-AHEAD-OF-THE-BALL ATTACKS?

Pivot and four man weave; post and four man roll; double post attack; pivot and post attack; double pivot attack; two-three attack; and three-two attack.

WHAT STYLES EMPLOY BALL-AHEAD-OF-THE-MAN?

Quick break (fast break); pressing offenses; Eastern style (give and go); figure eight; and practically all zone attacks.

ARE THERE ANY OTHER ATTACKING STYLES?

Yes. Attacks known as figure or pattern offenses incorporate both man-ahead-of-the-ball and ball-ahead-of-the-man principles.

With the above introduction to the principles underlying most basketball attacks, the beginning coach may be better prepared to analyze the formations and plays which follow in this book. It is wise to keep in mind that the delayed attack is classified into three styles of play: Free Play, Figure and Pattern Attacks, and Set Formations. Each is covered and identified in this book. Naturally, there are a great many variations of these basic attacking philosophies and it is here that the coaches differ in the presentation of their team attacks. These differences are found not only in the formations they employ, but in the personnel they assign to the various positions, the timing of the plays, in the use of set or moving post and pivot players, and in the maneuvers and player-paths which lead to the scoring of the basket.

The style of play known as "Eastern" basketball, employing give-and-go tactics; single, double and triple post or pivot formations, and practically every conceivable combination of pattern, figure and/or set position formation will be found outlined. In addition, treatises on the Quick Break, Out-of-Bounds plays, Jump Ball plays, and a special section devoted to attacking the basic zone defenses are included. Good luck!

INFORMATION CHART

In the interest of uniformity and for the purposes of this book, the legends and diagram keys described below have been applied to all of the material submitted.

ATTACKING PLAYER ◯   DEFENDING PLAYER ▢   PATH OF PLAYER ————————▶

BALL ⬤   PATH OF BALL —▶—▶—▶   PATH OF DRIBBLER ∿∿∿∿▶

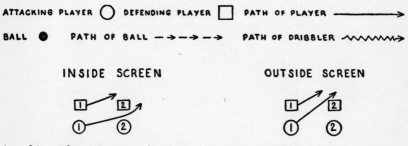

INSIDE SCREEN	OUTSIDE SCREEN

Attacking Player 1 moves between his teammate 2 and 2's opponent, defending player 2.

Attacking Player 1 moves behind his teammate's guard, defending player 2.

An attacking player stationed on the free-throw line or near this line with his back to the basket is termed a Post player.

An attacking player stationed beside or near the basket facing the rear court is termed a Pivot player.

Part I

ATTACKING THE MAN-TO-MAN DEFENSE

(Every conceivable attack known in basketball against the man-to-man defense.)

Part 1

FORREST C. (Phog) ALLEN
University of Kansas

Phog Allen, dean of American court tutors, justifiably takes the lead-off position in this book. Forty years of experience in any sport is unusual and active participation in one for that length of time is phenomenal. But, those of you who know the good doctor, know that the impossible is just a push-over where he is concerned.

He has made countless contributions to basketball through research on different phases of the sport and through his years of activity. He was one of the founders of the National Coaches Association, has served several seasons on the National Rules Committee, and was instrumental in founding the N.C.A.A. tournament. His efforts toward such innovations as rotation of the center jump, fan-shaped backboards, and a 12-foot basket are nationally famous.

Outstanding among Allen pupils who are famous in basketball coaching are Lonborg at Northwestern, Cox at Colorado, and Adolph Rupp of Kentucky. Scores of famous Jayhawkers have made their mark in basketball because of the expert instruction they received from Phog.

Allen still dons a full suit for most of his club's workouts, demonstrating shooting, passing, guarding and other fundamentals of the game. In his playing days, Phog was manager of the famous Kansas City Athletic Club which upset the world champion Buffalo Germans in a three-game series in 1905. Phog's "Stratified Transitional Man-for-Man Defense with the Zone Principle" is confusing to most experts but it is effective.

The University of Kansas Basketball Offense

With very few exceptions, the University of Kansas offense stations each of the two offensive forwards ten feet from the endline and about ten feet from each sideline. The other three offensive men are stationed approximately eight feet in front of the division line, with the center (3) in quarter-back position and the two offensive guards about ten feet to each side of him and about ten feet from each sideline. Owing to the 10-second rule requirement, all players are in the front or offensive court.

In this set offensive formation the ball can be snapped back and forth from guard to center to guard to center to guard, as opportunities present. As an aid to clarity, these various plays are numbered, but in a game situa-

3

tion numbers are not necessary. Any one of the rear three men who is holding the ball, namely the center or either of the two guards, may initiate the play.

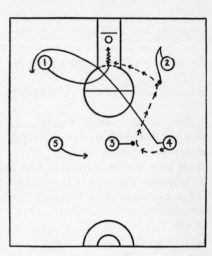

Play 1

Offensive player 4 whips the ball to 3 and cuts in front, calling for the return pass. Just after 4 crosses in front of 3, player 3 chest-passes to 2 who breaks to the ball. Simultaneously, player 4 continues to the opposite corner of the court to screen player 1's guard. Player 1 then cuts out in front and around 4. Player 2, in catching the ball from 3, takes one step forward, turns on his outside foot, pivots in the air, and snaps the ball overhead with a looping pass to 1 who cuts in for a dribble or a shot. Players 5 and 3 slide in the direction vacated by 4.

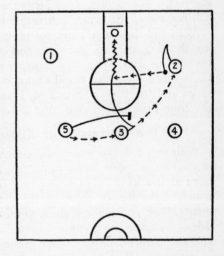

Play 2

Player 5 snaps the ball to 3 and screen-blocks as shown. Player 3 snaps the ball to 2, who comes up to meet the pass. After 3 bounce-passes to 2, he cuts to his left and behind 5's screen to receive a return pass from 2. Player 3 then dribbles on into the basket for a shot. Of course, in order to insure a high degree of efficacy for this play, 3's guard should be crowding the play. The guard who plays back at a sizable distance cannot have this return pass worked on him.

Play 3

This play may be used advantageously immediately after Play 1. The offensive guard (4) has the ball, and snaps it to 3. Player 3 snaps the ball to 2 who meets the pass. Player 3 then drives toward the free-throw line, calling for a return pass. Player 2 catches the ball and dribbles out and in front, about four steps, and fake-passes to 3, who feints to drive in. Just at this juncture, 4 drives forward and in, toward the dribbling player 2. After 4 has gone in about four steps,

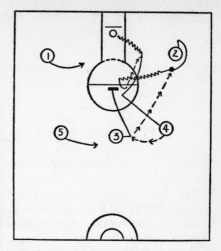

he quickly cross-steps and swings out and around behind player 2, who pivots and hands the ball to 4, who dribbles in to the goal.

Play 4

The center (3) feints a pass to 1 and then floor-bounces to 2. Player 2 comes up aggressively and, with the proper timing, receives the ball. Now, player 3 quickly starts forward and laterally to screen 4. Following this, player 2 passes to 4 who has cut forward to a position near the free-throw circle. Player 4, aided by the splendid screening of 3, has been freed of his opposing guard, and now dribbles on into the basket for a goal.

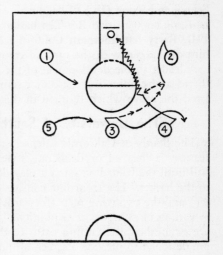

JUSTIN (Sam) BARRY
University of Southern California

Sam Barry went to Troy in 1930 from the University of Iowa. Excluding the war years, Barry has been head baseball and basketball coach ever since, also holding the job of assistant football coach. Under his leadership, Trojan basketball teams have won five P.C.C., Southern Division titles and three P.C.C. playoff championships. In three other years, his teams tied for the Southern Division crown, only to lose in playoff games.

Troy's mentor was an all-around athlete at Lawrence (Wis.) College where he starred in football, baseball and basketball. He later attended the University of Wisconsin and then coached at Madison (Wis.) High School and Knox (Ill.) College where he was director of athletics. At Iowa he came up with two Big Ten basketball titles (ties) in 1923 and 1926. In 1941, Barry left Southern California for a hitch in the Navy, which saw him discharged with the rank of commander.

A leader in the development of the cage sport, it was he who originated the idea of eliminating the center jump after every basket. He also stimulated the move which resulted in the adoption of the 10-second rule.

The University of Southern California Offense

The Southern California offense stresses ball control and steadiness and features a delayed or deliberate style of attack. The guards control the ball until the front line starts a play designed to open up a good shot close to the basket. The front line consists of a pivot operator (usually the center) and the two wing men (forwards) who originate each play by moving to various blocking spots or positions. When the blocking posts or positions are established, the cutting paths of the front line wings or of the guards are designed to provide a screen around or behind which a teammate may drive for the basket and a score. The center (pivot player) plays a vital part in this attack, being used chiefly as a legal blocking post. His part in the team scoring usually results from his follow-in ability, although he may be called upon for direct pivot or turn shots if he possesses unusual skill in the use of this weapon.

Variations in the basic plan of attack permit the guards to originate plays by passing and assuming cutting paths which incorporate inside and outside screens as well as the use of simultaneous cutting to opposite sides of the basket by the two guards (the scissors cut).

6

Basic Formation

The formation used at Southern California might well be called a Two-Two-One. (Two guards in the backcourt line, two forwards or wing men in a second line with the center or pivot man in the third line working in or near the basket and occasionally moving to the free-throw line.) In the diagram above 4 and 5 are the backcourt operators in charge of the ball. Players 2 and 3 are the wing men in the second line, while 1 occupies the front line position.

Play 1

The play is set up for 2. Player 4 passes to 5 and half screens, as shown. Player 5 passes to 3 who meets ball, then 5 drives behind 4 and sets up block on left side of free-throw lane. Player 1 moves to a position on the free-throw lane beside 5. Player 2 times his cut to take advantage of double block by 5 and 1, drives three steps toward basket and then changes direction and cuts around 5 and receives the ball from 3.

Play 1A

This alternate is designed to free player 1 if his guard has been switching to stop 2 in Play 1. All moves follow Play 1 pattern until 2 starts his drive for the basket. When 2 sees 1's guard start to switch, he stops behind 5. Player 1 cuts around the double block set up by 5 and 2, and receives the ball from 3.

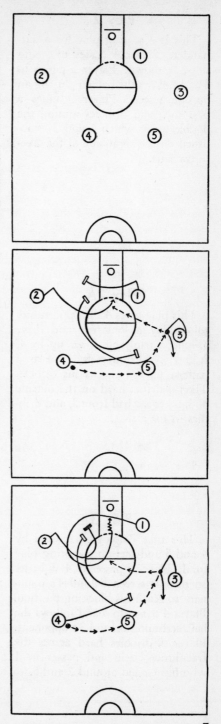

7

Play 2

This is a scoring play for a left-hander. Player 4 passes to 5 and stops as shown. Player 5 passes to 3 and follows the ball employing an outside screen. Player 3 fakes a pass to 5 and dribbles around the double block which 1 and 2 established on the right side of the free-throw lane.

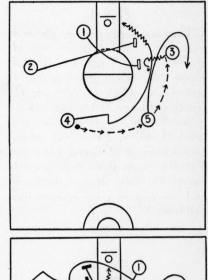

Play 2A

This play gives 4 the opportunity to employ a long cut and drive around a triple block set up by 1, 2, and 3. All moves follow Play 2 pattern until 3 checks his dribble. Then 4 drives hard on the outside of 3, takes the ball from 3, and dribbles in for a shot.

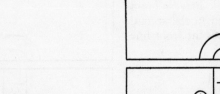

Play 3

This play employs a scissors by 4 and 5 and sets up a scoring play for 1. Player 5 passes to 4 and uses an outside screen behind 4's opponent to reach his blocking position. Player 4 passes to 3 and follows the ball, screening behind 3's opponent. Player 3 dribbles hard across the free-throw circle and passes to 1 who has circled around 2 and 5.

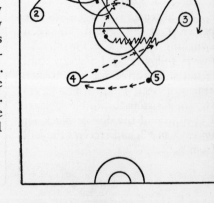

Play 3A

This is a scoring play for 2. Player 5 starts the play by passing to 4 and cutting to the left side of the free-throw lane. Player 4 passes to 3, who dribbles to the left and returns the ball to 4. Player 2 and 1 move simultaneously, 1 establishing a block on the left side of the lane, while 2 cuts across the free-throw circle and moves slowly down the right side of the lane. When 2 reaches the basket, he puts on speed and circles around 5 and 1 to receive the ball from 4.

Play 4

This is a scissors and double-block scoring play for 5. Player 1 breaks to a post position on the free-throw line receiving the ball from 4, who follows the pass and cuts as shown. Player 2 sets up a block at the junction of the lane and free-throw circle. Player 5 scissors as close behind 4 as possible and receives the ball from 1 and dribbles around 2 and in to the basket.

Play 4A

Player 4 again passes to 1 who receives the ball at the free-throw line. Player 2 sets up a block as shown. Player 4 cuts to the right of 1. Player 5 again scissors close behind 4 and around 1 and 2. Player 1 fakes a pass to 5 as he cuts by and then passes to 3. Player 5 continues on around 2 and under the basket where he receives the ball from 3.

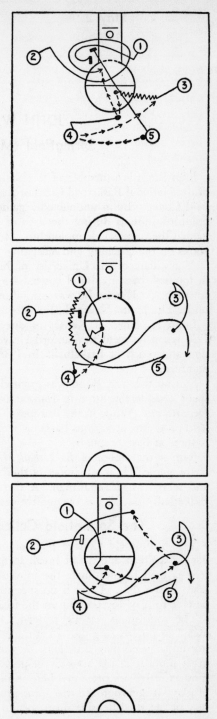

JOHN W. BUNN
Springfield (Mass.) College

John Bunn is a member of the National Rules Committee and an officer of the National Basketball Coaches Association. Currently coach at Springfield College, Bunn undoubtedly gained most prominence as coach of the Stanford Indians during the days of Hank Luisetti and the team which gained the national championship. Mr. Bunn is the author of a number of books on the coaching and officiating of basketball.

A graduate of the University of Kansas, Bunn won ten varsity letters in football, basketball and baseball—a record which still stands at that institution. At Kansas, he was a pupil of Phog Allen. Later, Bunn did work under Dr. James Naismith, inventor of basketball.

Bunn remained at Kansas as director of all basketball activities until 1930 when he went to Stanford University as professor of physical education and coach of basketball. In 1938 he was appointed dean of men at Stanford.

During the war, Bunn was granted a leave of absence by Stanford and spent considerable time in Europe as an athletic consultant for the War Department. While in the European Theater, he aided in establishing athletic programs at various bases, as well as inaugurating rehabilitation procedures at base hospitals.

John is the author of *Basketball Methods* which is a standard textbook of the game. He is a member of the National Basketball Rules Committee and served as vice-chairman. A member of the National Association of Basketball Coaches for twenty-five years, he was elected president in 1949.

The Springfield College Offensive Pattern

The Springfield College plan of offense is woven about a continuous passing pattern and a fast break formation. The continuous passing pattern is used to coordinate the movements of all players and to weld the team into a unit. There is no specialization by any player and each must be able to play any position in the formation.

The continuous passing pattern serves as a method of playing "keep-away" or for freezing the ball at the end of the game as well as for developing unbalanced play situations for various defenses. Out of the pattern, a great number of plays are developed. Those which have proved to be the most effective are presented here to illustrate the application of the system of play. It is recognized that some preliminary maneuvering may be necessary before the offensive thrust begins.

Continuous Pass Pattern

(The diagram numbers indicate the order of movement (timing) of the ball as well as the players.)

CONTINUITY: 1—(5 passes to 4), 2—(2 moves to ball), 3—(4 passes to 2), 4—(4 cuts to corner), 5—(1 moves to right of basket), 6—(5 breaks to left side of backcourt), 7—(2 passes to 5), 8—(1 breaks to free-throw line), 9—(5 passes to 1 at free-throw line), 10—(3 moves to backcourt), 11—(1 passes to 3), 12—(1 moves to right side of court). If no play has developed, the continuity is repeated.

Play 1

This play is set up for player 1. 1—(5 passes to 4), 2—(2 fakes to his right and breaks back toward 4), 3—(4 passes to 2), 4—(4 breaks to the left corner), 5—(2 passes to 4 in the corner and at the same time 1 cuts to the right side of the lane and waits for 2's screen), 6—(2 drives toward basket), 7—(1 cuts behind 2 to the left side of lane), 8—(4 passes to 1 under basket).

Play 1A

This is a scoring play for player 4. 1—(5 passes to 4), 2—(2 fakes to his left and breaks back toward 4), 3—(4 passes to 2), 4—(4 cuts to left corner), 5—(2 passes to 4), 6—(2 cuts to right corner), 7—(1 swings in circle across lane and back to left), 8—(5 moves to left side of court), 9—(4 passes to 5), 10—(4 starts toward basket as 3 breaks out), 11—(5 passes to 3), 12—(3 passes to 4 who is driving hard for basket behind 1).

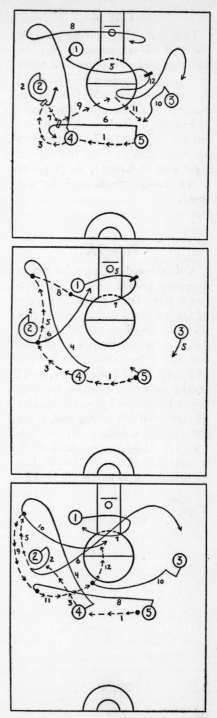

Play 2

This is another scoring play for player 4. 1—(5 passes to 4), 2—(2 fakes toward corner and turns back), 3—(4 passes to 2), 4—(4 cuts to left corner), 5—(1 moves to right side of lane and then breaks to free-throw line), 6—(5 moves to left side of court), 7—(2 passes to 5), 8—(4 cuts to pivot position on right side of basket), 9—(5 passes to 1), 10—(1 passes to 4 for the shot).

Play 2A

A dribble-scoring play for player 5 cutting off the post at the free-throw line. 1—(5 passes to 4), 2—(2 fakes toward basket), 3—(4 passes to 2), 4—(4 cuts to left corner), 5—(1 moves to right side of lane and waits), 6—(5 moves to left side of court), 7—(2 passes to 5), 8—(1 breaks to a post position on free-throw line), 9—(5 passes to 1), 10—(4 cuts from left corner and, at the same time, 3 screens across the circle for 5), 11—(5 cuts behind 3's screen), 12—(1 hands off to 5), 13—(5 dribbles in to basket for shot).

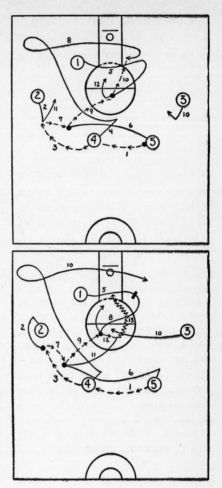

HOWARD G. (Jake) CANN
New York University

Jake Cann was undoubtedly the greatest all-around athlete in New York University history. While he showed to great advantage in basketball, he was also a prominent member of the Violet football and track teams. In 1917 he was captain of the basketball team and 1919 leader of the football eleven. He starred as a forward on the court and stood out both as a tackle and fullback on the gridiron.

His exploits in the National A.A.U. basketball championship tournament in Atlanta, Georgia, in 1920, in which he scored thirty-two field goals to help N.Y.U. win the national crown, earned him the award as the "greatest basketball player in the world." He was also chosen All-America forward that year.

He won the I.C.A.A.A.A. shot-put championship in 1920 and the Middle Atlantic States crown in this event the same year. He was chosen as a member of the American Olympic team which competed in Antwerp.

He entered the College of Engineering of N.Y.U. in 1915 and left in 1917 to enlist in the U. S. Navy. Graduating in 1920, Jake assisted in coaching basketball and football and has been with the Violets ever since. In addition to his coaching activities, Cann serves as the director of physical training, with the rank of associate professor.

His coaching record at his alma mater for the past twenty-five years shows 320 victories and 138 defeats. In 1933-34 the Violets went through a season of sixteen games undefeated and in 1934-35 bowed only once on a 21-game schedule. The 1944-45 outfit won the Eastern N.C.A.A. Championship; the 1947-48 aggregation were runners-up in the National Invitation Tournament; and the succeeding team participated in the 1948 Olympic trials.

New York University's Basic Formation Number I.
(Figure Eight)

In outlining two basic formations, it should be clearly understood that these formations are adopted only after the fast break has been attempted or is impossible. These formations are (1) The Figure Eight, and (2) The Single Pivot.

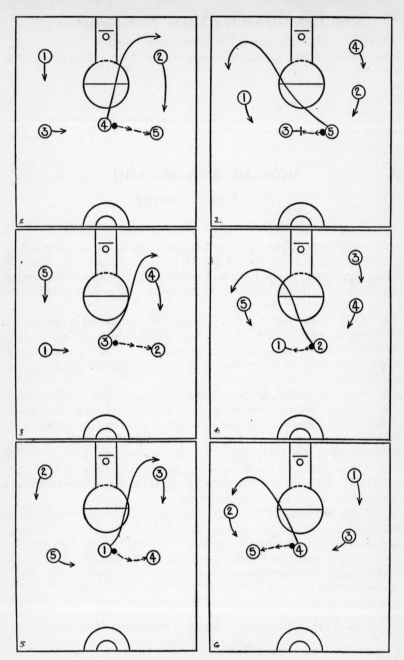

Figure Eight Formation

Movement of the players on this formation is easily followed by noting the change of positions by 1, 2, 3, 4 and 5.

New York University's Single Pivot Formation

In this formation, the center is not necessarily used as the pivot man although he is in that position more often than any other player. The guards (4) and (5) are in charge of the backcourt and if a play calls for them to cut through they are replaced by the forwards (2) and (3). A tall forward (3) is stationed in one of the corners and frequently replaces the center (1) in the pivot position. This forward is important in the screening which takes place in the front court and for follow-in work. The other forward assists the guards in starting the plays.

Out of this formation, we have built up countless numbers of good plays, many of which are optional with the players as situations develop. The formation provides backcourt protection or defensive balance when the ball is lost.

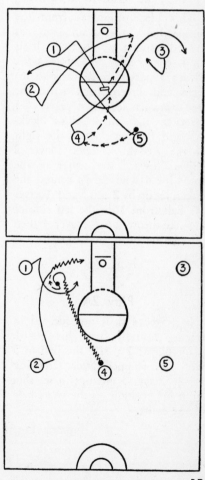

Split-the-Post Play

A simple split-the-post play showing movement of the players in the circulation used in the single pivot formation. Player 5 passes the ball to 4 and screens for 4 and 2. Pivot player 1 breaks to a post position on the free-throw line. After receiving the ball from 4, 1 bounce-passes to 2 for the scoring attempt. Player 3 follows-in.

Play 1. Moving Pivot

This play starts with three men in the backcourt and a man in each corner. Player 4 dribbles to a sliding pivot position in the left corner. As soon as 4 arrives at the pivot position, 1 cuts around 4 and drives toward the basket. Player 4 fakes a pass to 1 and waits for 2 who times his cut to break close behind 1. Player 4 passes to 2 who cuts or dribbles in to the basket for a shot.

Play 1A

In Play 1, the defense may or may not switch to stop the split-the-post tactics of 1 and 2. However, should the defense fail to switch to cover 1 but cover 2, 4 can again fake the pass to 1, give the ball to 2, and drop back for a good set shot position. After receiving the ball from 4, 2 can dribble once or twice and then return the pass to 4 who can attempt the shot.

Play 2. Guard Around

This play originates from the Single Pivot formation and has proved especially effective. It is used consistently to both sides. Player 5 passes to 1, starts to his right and screens back across the free-throw circle. Pivot player (1) meets the ball and sets up a blocking and feeding post at the right of the free-throw line. Player 2 screens toward the center of the court for 4 who drives behind the screen set up by 2 and 5 and receives the ball from 1 on the left side of the free-throw lane. Player 4 then dribbles on in to the basket for the shot.

Play 2A

If player 4 does not succeed in freeing himself from his guard, pivot player 1 passes the ball to 5 who has stopped after screening for 4. Player 5 attempts a set shot from his position on the weak side of the court.

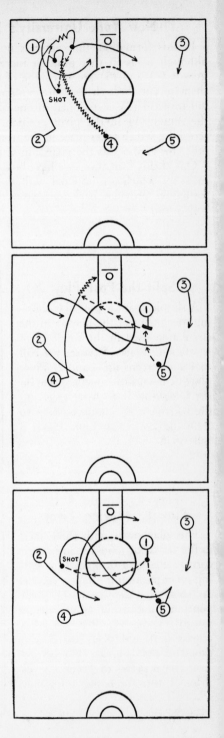

Play 3. Set Screen

Success depends upon proper timing, passing and cutting. The center of the court must be kept open. Player 2 passes to 1 and cuts diagonally across the free-throw circle. Player 1 meets the ball and passes to 3 who has moved to a post position on the free-throw line. Player 4 screens across the court toward the right sideline for 5 who fakes to his right and drives behind 4. Player 5 then stops on the left side of the free-throw lane. Player 3 passes to 5 for the shot.

Play 3A

This alternate play is used often to confuse scouting notes. Player 2 again passes to 1 and cuts diagonally across the free-throw lane toward the right corner. Player 4 again screens for 5 who cuts as shown. Player 3 again breaks to the free-throw line, receives the pass from 1, fakes the pass to 5, and then hands off to 1 who cuts from the left corner and around in front of him. Player 1 then dribbles on in to the basket for a shot.

Play 4. Single Post

This play works well against teams which employ a tight backcourt defense. Player 1 assumes a post position on the free-throw line. Player 4 starts the play by passing to 5 and stepping toward 5. Simultaneously, 2 and 3 break out toward 4 and 5 to set up moving screens. Player 5 passes to 1, starts to his left and cuts to the right of the post player (1). Player 4, on his side of the court, does likewise. Player 1 passes to either man who gets the step on his opponent.

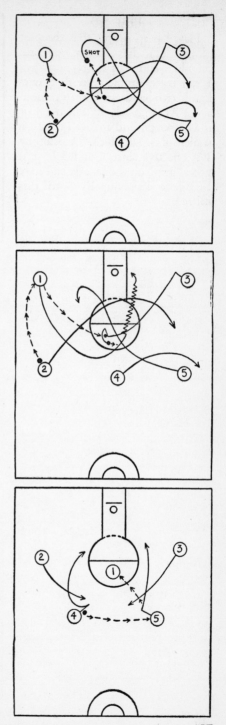

Play 4A

Play 4 is so simple that the post player (1) has many options. Should 4 and 5 be closely guarded, 1 can try a simple turn shot, one-hand, two-hand set shot, or jump shot. Alternatively he can use 4 or 5 as a screen and follow in with a trailer play (dribble). A shot by 1 is effective since 4 and 5 have a good "grip" on the boards and may be able to double up 1's shot if it is missed.

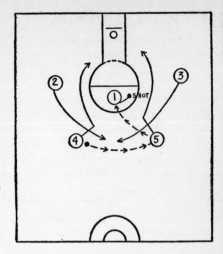

DR. HAROLD C. (Red) CARLSON
University of Pittsburgh

Red Carlson has compiled an enviable record as an athlete, coach, and student health director at the University of Pittsburgh. Born in Murray City, Ohio, Carlson became a Pennsylvanian at the age of two. He graduated from Fayette City High School, Bellefonte Academy, and went on to the University of Pittsburgh where he won twelve letters, playing as a regular for four years in three sports. While continuing his medical education (he has an M.D. degree) he played professional football with Cleveland and also helped coach at Mars High School.

Carlson was named freshman baseball coach at Pittsburgh in 1920, coached a year of football at Braddock High School, and then became freshman football coach at Pitt in 1922. More important, he took over the basketball reins that same winter as head court mentor, starting his long career as one of the country's outstanding coaches.

In 1932 Carlson became a full-time member of the University's administrative staff as director of men's student health services. In this capacity he has done extensive experimenting with the effects of fatigue and the best means of combating it. He has found that his players compete to better advantage when they go all out for short periods of time with frequent rests than if they pace themselves through the entire game.

His record as a coach speaks for itself. His teams have won 323 games and lost 187 in the past twenty-six years. He has developed three All-America players, but not once has he advocated rules changes. His famous continuity system (the figure eight) brought inquiries from all over the United States and resulted in his first book, *You and Basketball.*

Carlson's Figure Eight in Continuity

In Carlson's famous Figure Eight in Continuity, three players are active while two are in comparative rest. While three figure eight continuities are used, each is adaptable for two locations on the court, and the number of continuities can therefore be considered six.

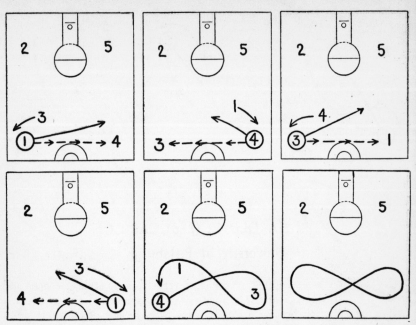

Continuity No. 1. This continuity works cross floor directly under or near the basket and in the backcourt near the 10-second line.

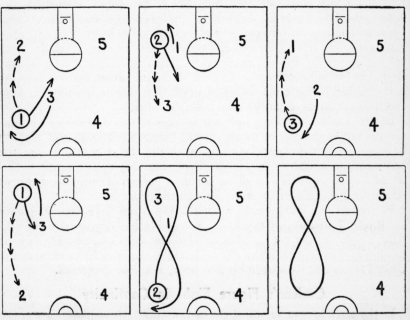

Continuity No. 2. This continuity works on the right and left side of the offensive court and lengthwise between the center of the court and the sideline.

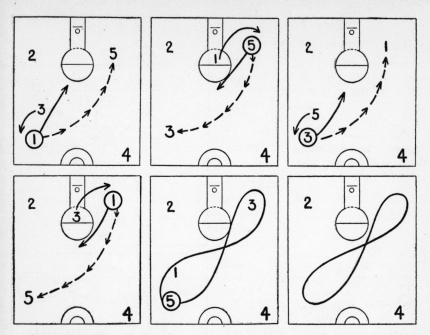

Continuity No. 3. This is a diagonal continuity working from left to right or right to left across the free-throw circle or lane.

In each of the foregoing, continuity is established by observing two simple rules which make the outlines especially attractive in physical education classes.

I. Pass the ball and cut toward the basket.
II. Replace your receiver *when* he becomes a passer.

A second continuity can be worked out as follows:

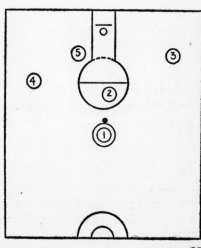

Basic Formation No. 1

One man out, four men in, including pivot man (5). Enclosed circle indicates location of the ball.

Play 1

Player 1 passes to 3 and cuts for the basket to receive a return pass for a shot at the basket. Pivot (5) goes to the opposite side of the basket from the wing man receiving the pass. Player 3 can pass to 1, 5, 4, or back to 2 (new backcourt man) either for a long shot or for the start of a new play.

The second continuity on the opposite side of the court:

Play 2

When 2 passes to 1, the arrows indicate the possibilities of the same plays on the opposite side of the floor from the first side pass. Player 1 may pass to 2, to 4, to 5, or pass to 3. The continuity comprehends passes between the backcourt man and the wing men for various plays or to the pivot man (5) for pivot play combinations.

Basic Formation No. 2

Two men out, three men in, with no stationary pivot man.

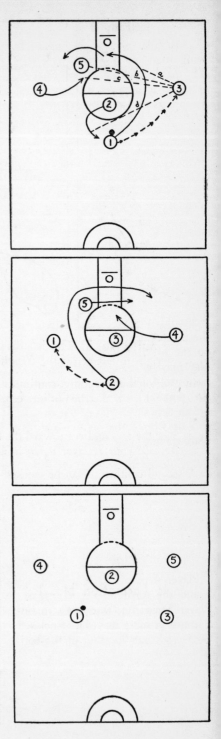

Play 1

This first play is to same-side wing man for a return pass (a). The passer-out replaces the passer. If the play appears no good, then 4 can pass to 2 (b), or to 3 (c).

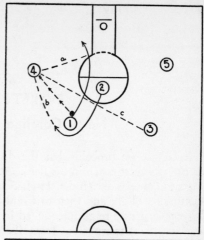

Play 2

Should 4 pass the ball to 2 in the preceding play, 4 will replace 2 on the free-throw line and a pivot play may be inaugurated. Player 2 passes to 4 and cuts to the right of the post. Player 3 does likewise on the left side. Player 4 may pass to 2 or 3 or to the players who replace them (1) or (5).

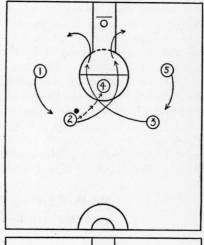

Play 3

Player 4 passes back to replacer 5 and the formation is as shown. Player 5 passes to wing man 3 for a return or for a new sequence.

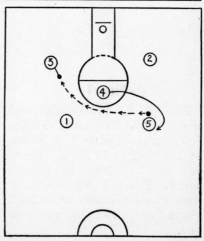

EVERETT N. CASE
North Carolina State University

Everett Case probably has the distinction of having started his career as the youngest coach in his field. At the age of eighteen he started coaching at Connersville (Ind.), High School. After a year there, he moved to Columbus High, and then to Frankfort High. At Frankfort, he began a 20-year coaching reign unequalled in Indiana. His Frankfort teams played in every state tournament from 1922 to 1931, winning the championships in 1925 and 1929. In all, he won the title four times (again in 1936 and 1939).

In the intervening years, Case spent two years at Anderson High School, coached the junior varsity at Southern California under Sam Barry, and coached the Firestone Californians, who won the all-Pacific A.A.U. title in 1933. In addition, he also coached the Hammond (Ind.) Cieasers in the National Professional League in 1941.

In 1942, Case was commissioned in the Navy and served as athletic director at the various bases to which he was assigned. In 1946, he assumed his duties as head coach at North Carolina State. In addition to acting as head coach of basketball at North Carolina State, Case annually conducts the Indiana State Coaching School, which he organized in 1926.

North Carolina State University's
Basic Three-Two Formation

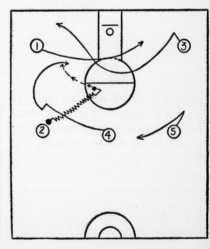

Play 1

Player 2 fakes a pass or shot, and after 4 screens 2's guard, 2 dribbles down the center of the floor. When he is stopped by 4's guard, 2 pivots and passes to 4 cutting for the basket. Player 1 cuts over and screens for 3, who cuts for the goal. Player 4 may shoot or he may pass to 3.

24

Play 2

Player 4 has the ball. He passes to 5, who meets the pass. Player 4 then screens 3's guard and 3 cuts toward the basket. Player 2 screens 1's guard. The pass goes from 5 to either 3 or 1. If the opponent's defense shifts on the screen, then 2 or 4 fade in.

Play 3

Player 4 has the ball and passes to 5. Player 5 passes to 3, and then cuts inside and screens for 3. At the same time, 1 comes down and screens for 2 who cuts behind 1 on the outside. Player 3 comes out with the ball on a short dribble and passes to 2. If 2 is not open on the screen because of a shift in defense, then 2 continues over and screens for 4 who made the initial pass, and 4 breaks around. In the event there is a shift on the defense after the screens, then the screener fades. The screener will be open nine times out of ten as he will be ahead of his defensive man on the shift of the defense.

Play 4

Player 5 has the ball and, as he gives the signal, 3 comes out and screens 5's guard. Player 5 dribbles in to the basket for a short shot if there is no shift of the defense. At the same time, 4 cuts over and screens for 2. Player 2 breaks through the center. If 5 is stopped, he may pass to 2. Player 1 fakes down the floor, reverses and breaks back fast.

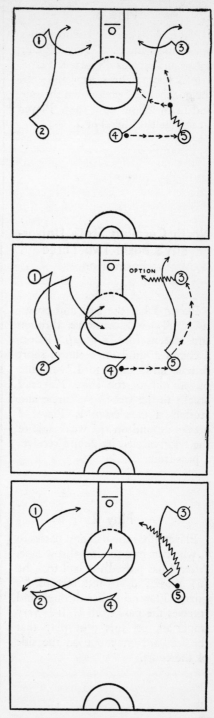

Play 5

Player 4 passes to 3 who comes out to meet the pass. Player 2 cuts across and screens 4's guard. Player 4 goes behind the screen and into the goal, while 5 goes down the side and in to follow up a shot. Player 3 can pass to either 4 or 5.

North Carolina State University's Basic Two-Three Formation

Play 1

Player 5 has the ball and passes to 3. Player 5 continues through and screens for 3's guard. Player 3 comes around on a sharp, short dribble and passes to 1, who has pulled out to the side. Player 2 breaks to the free-throw circle and receives a pass from 1. Player 4 breaks around on the weak side of the floor vacated by 2, and receives a pass from 2.

Play 2

Player 4 has the ball and passes to 1, who cuts into the free-throw lane. After 4 has passed the ball to 1, he (4) crosses over and screens 5's guard. Player 5 knifes through and receives the pass from 1. It is very important on this post play that the forwards stay out on the side of the court.

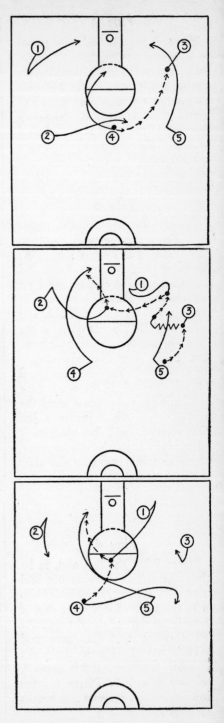

Play 3

Player 5 has the ball and passes to 1, who cuts into the free-throw area to receive the direct pass. Player 5, after passing the ball to 1, cuts across the floor and screens 4's guard. Player 4 cuts in, receives a pass from 1 and dribbles to the right of the free-throw circle. After 1 gives the ball to 4, he pivots quickly to his right and cuts toward the basket receiving the ball from 4.

Play 4

Player 1 comes out and screens 4's guard. Player 4 passes the ball to 5 and then screens 5's guard. Player 5 starts to dribble and 1 then goes over and screens for 2, who is open to receive the ball and take a set shot. This play may be worked on either side of the court.

Play 5

Player 4 passes to 5 after which he cuts across the floor and screens 3's guard. Player 3 comes around the screen and is open for a pass from 5. If there is no shift by defensive players, 5 passes to 2 across the court. Player 2 passes to 3 who has been freed by the screen.

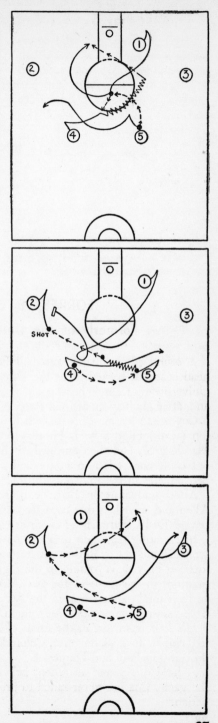

FORREST B. (Frosty) COX
Formerly of the University of Colorado

A sound education in basketball fitted Frosty Cox for the position of head coach of basketball at the University of Colorado in 1935. At the University of Kansas, he was an outstanding football and basketball star and, after graduation, assisted Phog Allen.

Cox began learning his basketball under Coach Frank Lindley at Newton (Kan.) High School. He played on Newton's championship teams of 1924-25-26-27, and then enrolled at the University of Kansas. An all-Big Six conference selection in football and basketball, Cox was one of the best athletes in the midlands during his undergraduate days.

After graduating in 1931, he became assistant basketball coach under Allen and served in that capacity until the summer of 1935 when he succeeded Earl Clark as head coach at Colorado.

In elevating Colorado to a top position in its sector, Cox's teams have won 127 and lost 69 in thirteen seasons. In his best season, 1942, the Buffaloes lost only to Wyoming in the regular 16-game schedule and bowed to Stanford in the finals of the N.C.A.A. Western play-offs at Kansas City. In their total participation in the N.C.A.A. Western play-offs, Cox's teams have won two games and lost four in three trips to Kansas City.

His 1938 team lost in the finals of New York's Invitation Tournament to Temple. In 1940, however, Colorado came back to win the Tournament, downing DePaul and Duquesne.

A hard driver and an ardent believer in teaching the fundamentals of the game, Cox has never failed to produce a pleasing, well-coached aggregation.

The University of Colorado's Double Post Attack

The Double Post attack developed by Frosty Cox employs a standard Three-Two formation with the two post men stationed in line with the free-throw stripe. Plays operate from either side of the court and each provides a number of options. The post ball handlers should be good one-hand marksmen and adept in follow-in ability.

Double Post Attack

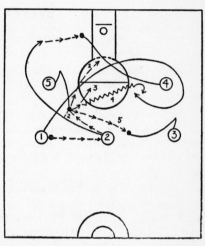

The Basic Double Post Attack with Options. Player 1 passes to 2 and cuts for the basket as shown. Player 5 moves out to receive the pass from 2. Player 4 uses 1, coming through as a "screener," and cuts for the basket (Option 1). Player 2 follows pass to 5 with a cut around to the outside (Option 2). Option 2 can also be a pass to player 4 under the basket in a pivot position. Option 3 is a fake pass to player 2, and a quick turn inside for a shot from the vicinity of the free-throw line. Option 4 is similar to Option 3. Player 5 drives to the free-throw circle but instead of taking the shot, 5 catches 1 driving around from the right side of the court and passes him the ball by means of a hand-off. Player 1 may shoot or dribble in to the basket. Option 5 is a pass out to 3 who has moved over to the center of the court. The formation is reset if none of the options open up.

Guard Around Play

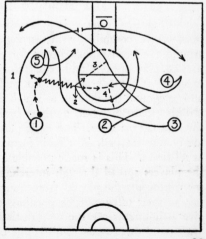

Player 1 passes to 5 and drives around the outside. Option is post player 5 passing off to 1. Player 2 moves over as the ball is passed and sets a screen for 3. Player 3 moves on around 5, who has dribbled up for Option 2. Player 2 uses the "Screen-go" on 3 and breaks for the option (3). Player 4 moves out behind the break of 2 for a pass from post player 5. Post player 5 follows his pass to 4 for Option 4. The formation is reset if none of the options open.

EVERETT DEAN
Stanford University

Everett Dean came to Stanford from Indiana University in 1938. While at Indiana, Everett coached baseball as well as basketball, winning three Big Ten titles in each sport.

After graduating from Indiana in 1921 with A.B. and A.M. degrees in Education, Dean coached basketball and baseball and assisted with football at Carleton (Minn.) College, for three years before returning to his alma mater. At Carleton, his basketball teams won forty-nine out of fifty-two games.

When Dean arrived at Stanford to take over the 1938-39 Indian team, the immortal Hank Luisetti and his teammates had graduated, leaving behind mediocre material. He spent two years building, and the third year paid off when Stanford won the P.C.C., Southern Division title. In 1942, his team repeated the performance and also added the N.C.A.A. championship.

In 1946, Dean was sent to Europe by the U. S. Army as civilian consultant on the athletic program for the Armed Forces. He is the author of *Progressive Basketball,* which is used by more than two hundred universities and colleges as a text. He is chairman of the research committee of the National Association of Basketball Coaches.

The Stanford University Offense

The Stanford offense is a versatile free-lance offense featuring a four-man weave combined with strong pivot play. Sometimes fast passing around the horn is substituted for the weave. This style provides many natural play options and equal scoring opportunities. The movement is executed at a moderate rate, but sufficiently fast to keep the offense alert and to compel the defense to watch their men in movement.

This offense has two or three basic plays from which many plays and their variations arise. The basic plays tend to hold the team together yet are not stereotyped. The basic formation provides for a good floor balance at all times. This is made possible because of the movement which keeps the players spread through interchanging positions. The weave or movement prevents the players from bunching and prevents them from getting lost in their offense. The positions are interchangeable since their defensive assignments are the only distinguishable differences between the forwards and the guards. This is one of the features that makes for equality in scoring opportunities. The pivot man and other players can interchange positions without affecting the movement of play.

This offense can be operated with either inside or outside screens. Double pick-offs and double-cutters are the main play possibilities. Some of the play options are shots from a screen or behind a screen; the "back door" play; cutaways or roll blocks on the side and out front between the guards; double-cutters off the pivot man; the double pivot; double- and triple-screens. The player with the ball is the playmaker and each player has the same responsibility in this respect. Almost all the plays are determined by the initiative of the player and the position of the ball on the floor.

It is imperative when using this offense that the squad be well grounded in the offensive fundamentals. Individual cleverness such as footwork, change of pace, change of direction, head, eye, shoulder and body fakes, clever deceptive passing and fine ball handling are essential to maximum efficiency in any offense. This offense will fail unless backed up with these fundamentals.

Play 1

Player 4 passes to 2 and screens. Player 2 dribbles and passes to center (1). Player 2 starts right and cuts left to pick-off for 4. Player 1 passes to open cutter. Players 5 and 3 interchange.

Play 2

Player 5 passes to 4 who passes to 1. Player 4 screens for 3 and they double-cut off the center (1). Player 1 gives ball to the open man. Player 3 may shoot or dribble in or set-screen on 5.

Play 3

Player 4 passes to 2 and screens. Player 1 pulls into play to open center for dribbler. Player 5 and 3 interchange to keep defense busy.

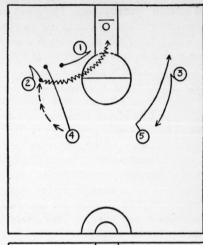

Play 4

Player 5 passes to 4, who passes to 2. Player 4 screens for 2, who dribbles across to the side of the pivot man who stations himself at the foul ring. Player 4 picks-off his guard on the double-block. Player 2 passes to 4, who stops behind block for shot or dribbles through the hole.

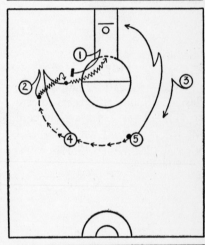

Play 5

Player 5 passes to 4; 4 passes to 2, while 5 cuts around 1 to double pivot post. Player 2 passes back to 4 who passes to 5. Players 4 and 2 double-cut off center. The center moves up for pick-off with 2 dribbling in.

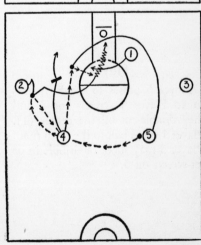

Play 6

Player 5 passes to 4, who dribbles and passes to 3. Player 3 passes back to 4 as he (3) picks-off 4's man, starting a roll-block for the basket. Player 1 pulls to opposite side.

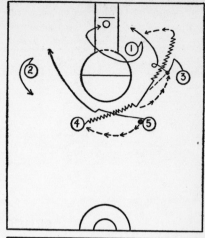

Play 7

Player 4 passes to 2. Player 2 fakes toward the free-throw line and reverses quickly. If the defensive center shifts to guard 2, then 2 will pass-off to 1. Player 1 may shoot or pass to 5 cutting in.

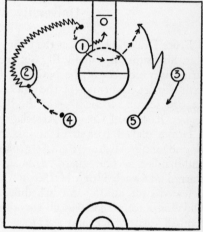

BRUCE DRAKE

University of Oklahoma

Bruce Drake is known as the man who seeks "suicide" schedules. Despite this, his teams are usually Big Six and N.C.A.A. championship contenders. Bruce is a member of the N.C.A.A. Basketball Rules Committee from the fifth district, chairman of the N.C.A.A. fifth district Basketball Selection Committee and a member of the board of directors of the National Collegiate Basketball Coaches Association.

Drake played basketball at Oklahoma and in 1929 made the Helms Foundation's All-America. As a player, Drake was a smooth passer and ball-handler, a fine guard, dribbler, shot-maker and team captain. He starred on Coach Hugh McDermott's great 1928 Sooner outfit that was undefeated over an 18-game schedule. In 1929, Drake captained a famous Oklahoma team that was all-victorious in Big Six play. Bruce was also a football quarterback and a 13-foot pole vaulter.

Drake's Oklahoma teams are noted for their careful organization, their smart passing, their emphasis upon ball control, their consistently brilliant free-throwing and tight guarding and their ability to vary their strategy for each opponent. As a coach, Drake is a bold strategist known for his keen plotting against opponents of national reputation. It was Drake, who in 1944, organized and led a national fight against goal-tending. Drake organized the nation's college coaches against it, 95 per cent of them voting to kill it, and the next year it was stricken from the rules.

The University of Oklahoma's Offense

In the eleven years Bruce Drake has coached at the University of Oklahoma he has never used the same offense twice. He depends upon a few situation plays, but his offense is never the same. Bruce finds it difficult to find boys that will make a set system go, so he feels it best to build an offense suitable to the material available.

The University of Oklahoma attacking theory is based upon the assumption that a defense is much easier to penetrate once it is moved from its original position. Therefore, the Sooner attack is developed so that it may have five or six scoring opportunities. The new positions gained on the failure of previous plays lead into further continuities, rather than to a return to the original starting positions. Drake further believes that a team which starts a play and then returns to the original starting position when the play fails, is working to the advantage of the defensive team. By continuing from positions gained on a given play however, the defense finds it difficult to anticipate the next movement of the opposition.

The plays which follow are the exact ones used by Oklahoma in winning the Big Seven championship in the 1948-49 season. The two formations with a little free-lance comprised the offense 100 per cent. Free-lance is used by Oklahoma from 25 to 40 per cent of the time.

In the single post plays, the post man is not vital to the operation of the plays. He can be hit if desired, but a sinking defense that would keep the ball away from the post man cannot keep the plays from getting under way.

Note, also, that it is virtually impossible for the weak side defensive man to give his teammates much help when the ball is on the other side of the court. This style is built on an overload pattern with plenty of baseline cuts derived from screens set up by men who had driven in toward the basket. It is simple to operate and all passes are easy to make. Drake uses this formation consistently in the second half when he has a commanding lead and chooses to play a bit more cautiously.

Oklahoma's three-two offense is used mainly against teams that either are not too strong defensively or who choose to press the front line. Bruce feels that the teams Oklahoma plays are more qualified to stop one formation than two. He believes, too, that his three-two attack permits better use of good set shot artists. It is also an offense that can be used to advantage when height is needed near the basket.

Single Post Play No. 1

Player 3 passes to 4 and 2 uses 3 on his cut past 5. Player 4 passes to 2 just before he gets even with 5. If 2's opponent floats behind 5, player 2 will stop and shoot over. If 2's man is sticking tight then he will try to go all the way. If he can't he will pass to 1 in the corner and the alternate play will follow. (Play 2)

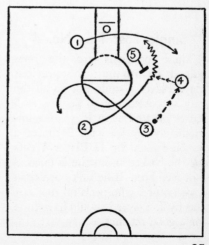

Single Post Play No. 2

As shown in Play 1, player 2 could not go all the way so he passes off to 1 who has moved over toward the corner. Player 1 passes out to 4 and screens for him. Player 4 passes to 5 who comes out to meet the pass and returns the ball to 4. Player 2 clears out to the corner as he makes the initial pass to 1.

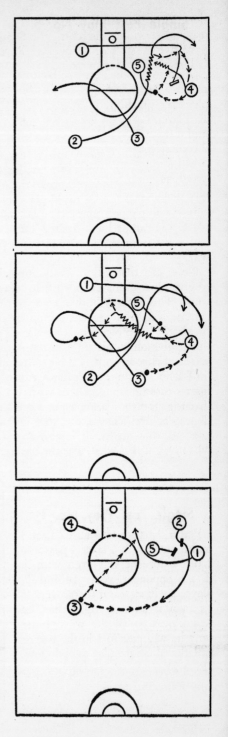

Single Post Play No. 3

This play starts just like Play 1, but player 4 instead of passing to 2, hits 5 who comes out just as 2 clears. Player 5 passes off to 4 who tries to go all the way to the basket. If 4 cannot get in, he passes out to 3. If he makes this pass, then the following play is run.

Single Post Play No. 4

These positions are the ones gained by running the previous play. Player 4 could not go all the way so passed out to 3. Just as 5 passes off to 4 as in Play 3, he immediately works with 2 to set a double-screen for 1. Player 1 cuts for the basket and, if he is open, 3 will feed him. If he isn't open then 3 looks for 2 who peels off just as 1 cuts by 5. Player 2 should have time for a good set shot.

Single Post Play No. 5

This sequence starts just like Play 3 except that player 5 does not pass off to 4 as he cuts by. Instead, player 5 feints a pass to 4 and dribbles over quickly and hands off to 1. Player 1 tries to go all the way and if he cannot, passes to 3. Player 2 comes on out on the "peel" using 5 as indicated in Play 4. The new positions are then assumed as shown in Play 4.

Single Post Play No. 6

Player 1 could not go all the way to the basket, so passed off as shown in Play 5. Player 3 passes to 2 who passes to 4 breaking out to the ball from behind the screen by 1. Then 2 peels behind 5.

Single Post Play No. 7

In the preceding plays, player 3 was used chiefly as an outlet for the man cutting for the basket. In this play he is the scorer. Player 5 sets the stage for this play by moving to the upper half of the circle when 2 has the ball. Players 2 and 3 split 5 with 5 handing off to 3. Player 3 tries to go all the way but if he cannot he veers to the left as shown in the following play.

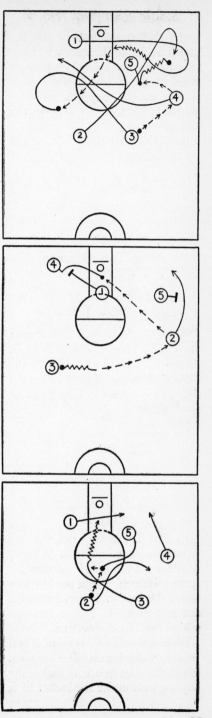

Single Post Play No. 8

Player 3 could not get to the basket, so he dribbles on out to the left. In the meantime, 4 has gone to the baseline and 1 has moved over to do the screening for him. Player 3 is looking for 4 under the basket.

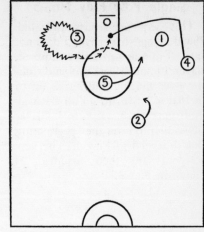

Three-Two Offense

Play 1

Player 3 passes to 5 and screens for 4 who takes the pass from 5. Player 3 is always run on 5. In the event 5 does not find 4 open, the alternate as shown in Play 2 will be possible.

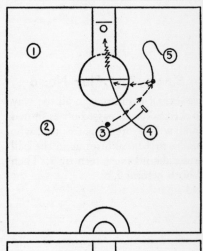

Play 2

In Play 1, Player 5 did not find 4 open so passed off to 3. When 4 does not get the ball, he screens for 1. If 1 is open, 3 will pass to him under the basket. If not, 3 dribbles out and passes to 5 at a spot opposite the free-throw line. Player 5 fakes a shot and passes to 2 and breaks to the basket off 1's screen. Player 2 passes to 4 who makes the feeding pass under the basket to 5.

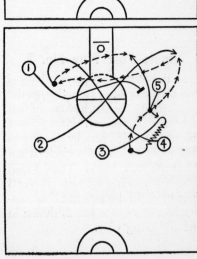

Play 3

Drake calls this a sneaker play. Player 3 passes to 4 and goes three-quarter speed down the middle to screen for 2. Player 4 holds the ball for a second, feinting a shot before he makes a pass to 5. Player 5 feeds 2. If opponents use a checking defense, player 3 should run down the slot.

Play 4

This is an alternate for Play 3. Player 5 does not find 2 open so passes out to 4. Player 5 goes over to screen for 1. Player 4 passes to 2 who will be looking for 1 cutting off 5's screen. Player 2 passes to 1 and if he is not open he looks for 4 who is screened by 2. (This is the old guard-around play.)

Play 5

This play is designed for a good set shot. Player 4 passes to 5 and screens for 3. Player 3 is looking for his long shot. If he is not open, we run the alternate as shown in the following play.

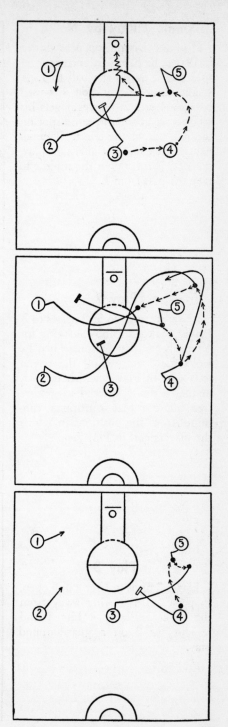

Play 6

If player 3 is not open as shown in Play 4, he passes ball across court to 2 and 2 passes the ball to 1. A staggered double-pick on 3 is used here by 4 and 2. Player 3 gets his set shot at about the same spot on the left side of the court. If opponents check on this alternate play, player 2 is run down the middle to take the pass from 1.

Play 7

Player 4 passes to 3; 3 passes to 2. Player 2 takes a dribble, looking for 4 who is the first option. Then he looks for 5 cutting off the screen set by 1. In Play 8 which follows, neither 4 nor 5 succeed in getting free but the play continuity continues from the positions in which the players end in Play 7.

Play 8

Player 2 finds neither 4 or 5 open, so passes to 4 moving away from the basket. Player 4 hits 5 and screens for 2 on a guard-around play.

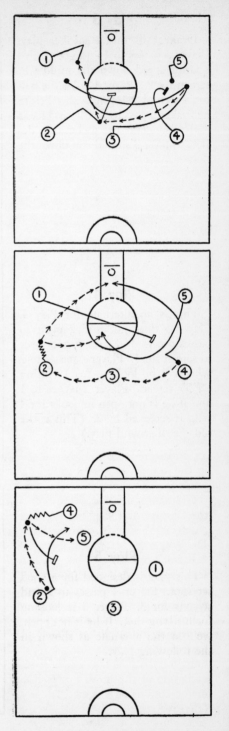

HAROLD E. (Bud) FOSTER
University of Wisconsin

Three Western Conference championships and one N.C.A.A. title in thirteen years of varsity coaching are the highlights in the career of Bud Foster. An outstanding player himself while a student at Wisconsin, Foster holds a place on the all-time list of Badger athletic greats.

Born in Newton, Kansas, on May 30, 1906, Bud prepared for college at Mason City, Iowa, and Chicago. He entered Wisconsin in 1926 and, while an under-graduate, majored in economics. He was all-conference at center in the seasons of 1929 and 1930, and also was named All-America in the latter season.

Graduating in June, 1930, Bud tried his hand at semi-pro basketball with the Chicago and Oshkosh teams until 1933, when he was named freshman coach at Wisconsin. He stepped into the varsity coaching position after Dr. Walter E. Meanwell resigned in July, 1934.

Foster's first Badger team tied for the conference crown, then came five lean years before he was able to weld a fine group of players into a winning combination during the 1940-41 season, which, after a poor start, won fifteen straight games to wind up as conference and N.C.A.A. champions.

Foster uses the fast break with his set formation plays and tries to have something to fit all defenses his team meets, including zones. He uses a basic shifting man-for-man defense, but has been using some zone combinations for the past few years. By using a regular play and a check play on each side of the floor, Foster has been able to throw as many as sixteen major options at a defense, depending upon their reactions to the general offensive style.

The University of Wisconsin's Continuity

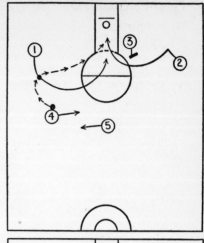

Play 1. Screen Criss-Cross

Player 4 passes to 1. As ball leaves 4's hand, 3 hits a post-screen for 2. Player 2 feints deep and cuts across in front of 3 to force a screen or cause a switch. Player 4, after passing, goes to top of arc. Player 5 crosses over to protect the ball. Player 1 passes to 2 and follows-in.

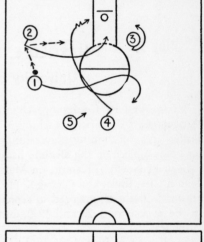

Play 2. Screen for Guard

If player 1 cannot pass to 2 in lane, player 2 continues to corner and 1 passes to him there. Player 1 after passing cuts across floor and 4 cuts off 1 for the screen. Player 2 passes to 4 cutting for the basket and follows the pass.

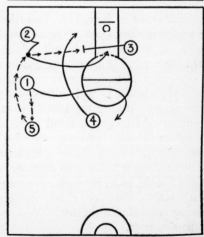

Play 3. Center Pivot Option

Player 1 throws ball to 5 and cuts across floor. Player 5 passes to 2. Player 2 passes to the pivot who meets the ball. Player 4 cuts behind the screens and joins 2 in splitting the pivot under the basket. (Player 5 may pass directly to the pivot (3) and players 2 and 4 cut as shown.)

Play 4. Guard Outside

Player 4 passes to 1 and holds until 1 throws fast pass to 3. As 1 passes, he throws outside foot with ball and holds a one-half pivot. Player 4 drives as foot of 1 comes down and cuts very tight to 1. Player 1 holds until 4 is past, then cuts in front of 3. Player 3 may pass to either 4 or 1, or he may shoot.

Play 5. Center Pivot from Side

Player 4 passes to 1 and holds at the side line. Player 1 spot-passes to 3 and follows tight. Player 2 comes from corner behind 1 on a scissors and cuts in front of 3. Defense is stacked on criss-cross and 3 passes to open man or shoots.

Play 6. Forwards Cross Post

Players 4 and 5 criss-cross with pass or dribble. Player 4 passes to 2 and screens inside while 5 is screening for 1. Player 2 passes to 3 on post and follows with 1 cutting behind. Player 3 may pass to best man, dribble in, or turn and shoot.

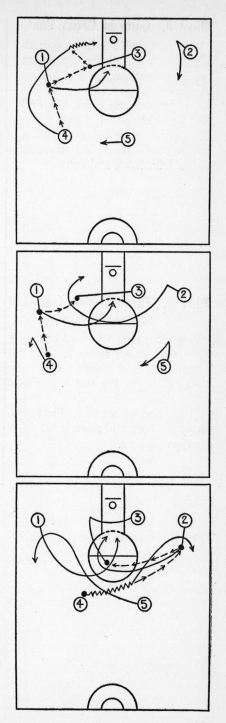

Play 7. Guards Cross Post

Players 4 and 5 criss-cross with dribble or pass. Player 4 passes to 3 on the free-throw line and follows his pass. Player 5 cuts to the left and reverses to the right. Player 3 may hit either guard or may shoot. (If opponents are using a shifting defense the guards cut through with a feint block and cut.)

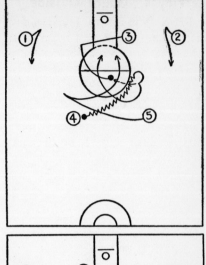

Play 8. Forward and Guard Cross Post

Player 5 passes to 3 and screens for 4 who drives through. Player 2 comes out and crosses post after 4 goes through. Player 3 may give ball to 4 for a drive-in shot, or pass to 2 for a short set shot. Player 3 may feint both and shoot if his opponent drops off.

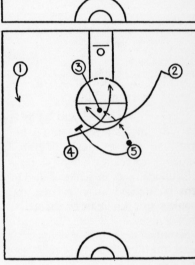

AMORY T. (Slats) GILL
Oregon State College

"Builder of men and maker of championship basketball teams," could well be applied to Slats Gill, Oregon State's veteran mastermind of the maple court. Gill's Beaver quintets have annexed more Northern Division crowns than any other league member.

Slats has been at the helm of Beaver basketball for more than twenty years, during which time they have won five Northern Division pennants and two Pacific Coast Conference titles.

First claim to fame for an Oregon State club came in 1933 when Ed Lewis and company romped to the coast title. Two years later, such outstanding players as George Hibbard, Wally Palmberg, Earl Conkling, Bob Bergstrom and Mose Lyman brought the Northern Division crown to State, only to lose a heartbreaker to the P.C.C. crown to Sam Barry's Southern California Trojans in the last fifteen seconds on a mid-court "prayer" basket by the late Ernie Holbrook.

In 1940, after a lapse of five years, Gill's protégés again achieved a Northern Division crown, but lost to Southern California in the coastal playoffs. The Beavers stormed back two years later (1942) to take the Northwest championship for the fourth time under Gill.

The Beavers, Gill-directed, are drilled in both zone and man-to-man defense, and use either a fast or slow break. A master strategist, and well-liked among the coaching corps of the entire nation, Gill is a credit to his profession.

Oregon State College's Two-Two-One Formation

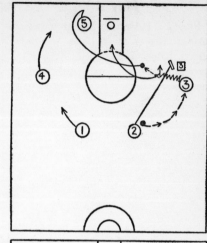

Play 1

Player 2 passes to 3, and screens inside on defensive 3. Player 3 dribbles by the screen and passes to Player 5 coming out to the post after the pass. Player 3 fakes outside and cuts inside around the post.

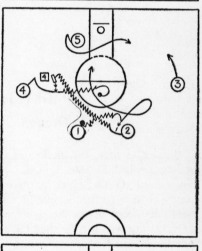

Play 2

Player 1 dribbles toward 2, hands back to 2, who dribbles toward 4, hands back to 4 who dribbles toward 1, makes front pivot and screens for 1.

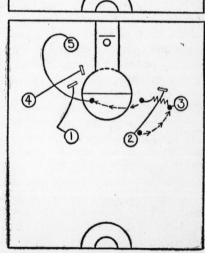

Play 3

Player 2 passes to 3 and screens 3. Player 3 dribbles by screen and passes to 5 coming around screen set by 1 and 4.

Play 4

Player 2 passes to 3, and screens inside. Player 3 dribbles around screen, passes to 5 on post. Player 1 screens inside for 3 as 1 and 3 split the post.

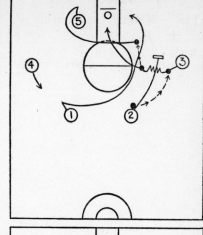

Play 5

Player 2 passes to 3 coming to outside post position. Player 2 breaks for 3 in such a manner as to cause 2 to be screened by 3. If 2 cannot get loose, 3 passes to 5 coming to a post position. Then 3 cuts to the left of 5.

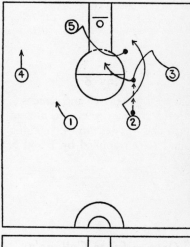

Play 6

Player 2 passes to 3 coming to an outside post. Player 2 then spreads taking pass from 3. After 3 passes, he moves to center of court and 2 passes to 5 on post and then drives by.

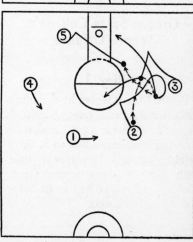

Play 7

Player 1 passes to 5 outside of foul line. Player 1 screens 2. After 2 takes advantage of the screen to cut to the left of 5, player 1 drives to the basket.

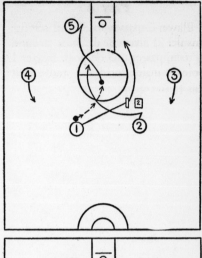

Play 8

Player 2 passes to 3 and screens 3. Player 3 dribbles toward center of court and passes to 4, coming around screen applied by 1 and 5.

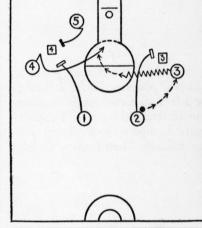

Oregon State College's Weave Offense

Play 1

Player 1 starts weave by dribbling ball toward 2 and handing back to 2. Player 2 dribbles toward 3 and, with a front pivot, hands ball to 3. As 3 dribbles toward 1, player 2 goes with him to apply screen on 1. Player 1 takes the ball from 3 for a drive to the basket.

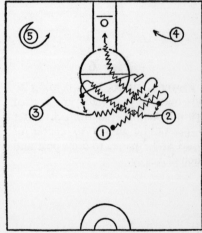

Play 2

Player 1 starts weave by dribbling toward 2. Player 2 dribbles toward 3, front-pivots as 3 goes by, but holds the ball and passes to 1 coming by screen applied by 3.

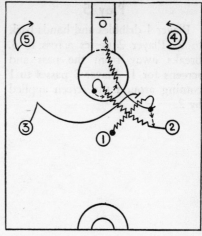

Play 3

Player 1 dribbles toward 2, hands the ball to 2. Player 2 dribbles to 3, who dribbles and passes back to Player 5 coming to the free-throw line as Player 2 screens 5.

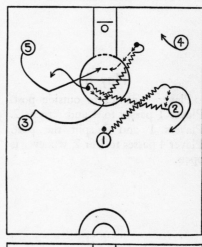

Play 4

Player 1 dribbles toward 2, passes back to 2, who dribbles and hands ball to 3, who dribbles toward right corner and passes to 5 coming to the post. After the pass, 3 fakes in and then goes around 5.

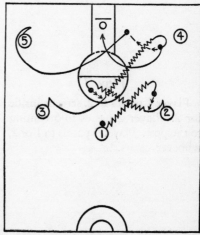

Play 5

Player 1 dribbles and hands back to 2. Player 2 passes across to 3, breaks away from the pass and screens for 1. Player 3 passes to 1 coming around the screen applied by 2.

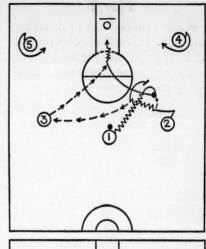

Play 6

Player 4 comes to outside post. Player 1 passes to 4 and screens 2. Players 1 and 2 split the post. Player 4 passes to 1 or 2, whoever is open.

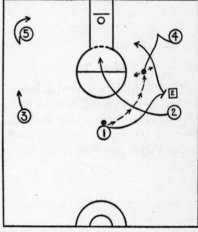

Play 7

Player 1 passes to 2, screens inside for 2. Player 2 passes to 5 coming to the post. Player 5 passes to 1 or 2, whoever clears.

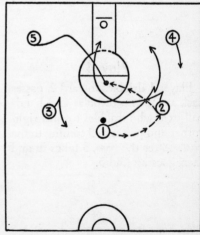

Play 8

Player 1 dribbles and hands back to 2. Player 2 dribbles and hands back to 3. Player 3 dribbles and screens 1 and hands ball to 1 going by.

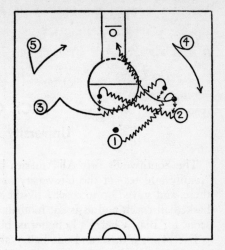

JACK GRAY
University of Texas

The Southwest's first All-America basketballer, Jack Gray is one of the "family athletes" at the University of Texas. He played there, graduated there, and stayed on to coach. By the time he was twenty-five he was head basketball coach and assistant football coach. In football, he serves as chief scout for Blair Cherry's Longhorns, but basketball is his principal concern.

Except for a three and one half year tour of duty with the Navy, mostly aboard Pacific Fleet aircraft carriers, Gray has been coaching basketball for the Steers since 1937. Although he had a national contender in 1939, he achieved his greatest successes in 1947, 1948 and 1949.

His season record of twenty-six won and two single-point losses made Texas one of the top three teams in the nation in 1946-47. Gray's successful gamble with a team of three "shorties"—all standing five feet, ten inches or less—won him acclaim throughout the coaching profession.

Short on material in the following year, he guided his squad to a season of twenty wins and five losses, despite having only six men play 85 per cent of all Texas' games! In the National Invitation Tournament, Texas drew the favorite, N.Y.U., in the opening round. The Longhorns came within inches of causing an upset but lost, 45-43, to wind up a two-season record of forty-six victories and seven losses.

The University of Texas' Offense

Wide Double Post

In this offense the player in No. 1 position always cuts toward the baseline and cuts from the baseline in the direction the original pass was thrown. Example: Player 1 passes to 3, 1 cuts toward baseline and rubs his man on 5 and is open for return pass from 3. If 1 passes to 2, 4 breaks to form double post and 1 rubs his man on 4 and opens for return pass from 2. This makes it possible to use a split on either post man.

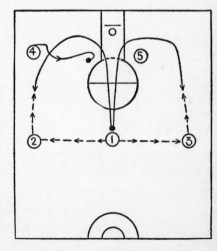

Single Post Play with Four-Man Roll

Post man 5 position is as indicated. Players 1, 2, 3 and 4 roll in a semicircle and not deeper than as indicated. Post man operates in different positions as indicated.

Split-at-Post Play

Player 1 passes to 3 and rubs man on 5. Player 3 passes to 1 who comes out to meet pass. Player 1 passes to 5 at post and breaks in front of 5. Player 3 breaks right off of 1, giving a split break on the post.

Split-at-Post Play 1A

If 1's man is playing tight and tries to prevent the rub on 5, then 1 passes to 3, breaks toward the base line, makes a false break to the left and then goes around 5 very close for the return pass from 3. Player 1 shoots over 5 or dribbles in for lay up.

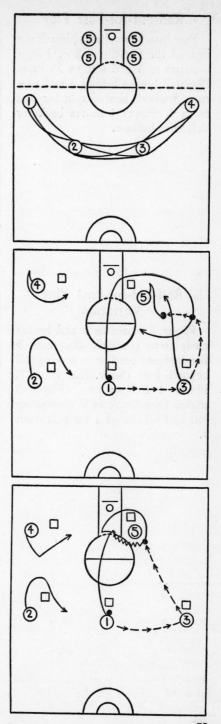

Roll-out-for-Post Play

Post man 5 establishes himself out beyond the free-throw line. Player 3 passes to 4 and screens 5's man. Player 2 breaks behind 3 and post man 5 wheels behind split for pass from 4. Player 1 moves back for defensive balance.

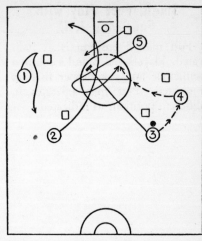

Roll-out-for-Post Play Variation

Player 2 passes to 1 and breaks away from the ball. Post man 5 breaks from baseline to receive ball beyond free throw line from 1. Player 1 follows pass. Player 3 makes false break as if continuing roll and breaks off 1 for pass from 5.

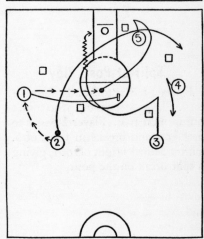

LAWRENCE (Pops) HARRISON
The State University of Iowa

Pops Harrison took over the head coaching job at the University of Iowa in 1942. Since then, he has guided Iowa to its Golden Age of basketball with a record which stands well above 78 per cent.

Harrison's first competitive basketball was played as a guard on the University High School team of Iowa City in 1924. At the University of Iowa, he was forward on the 1926 team, played forward again in 1926-27, and was a guard during his senior year, 1927-28. After his graduation from Iowa in 1928 he went to Westminster College in Pennsylvania for the 1929-30 season where his team lost but one game of thirty-one.

From Westminster, Harris went back to Iowa, in 1931, as a coaching assistant in basketball and baseball, taking over the head coaching spot in 1942-43. His 1944-45 team was the first in Hawkeye history to win a clear conference title. It won eleven of twelve conference games, emerging with a 17-1 record for the entire season.

Harrison's boys are coached to stick to their type of game, "whittling away" according to plan, no matter what the opposition tries. His players take plenty of shots and Harrison coaches them in sound, smart and fast basketball.

The State University of Iowa's Offense

Harrison's Iowa University teams are equipped with two distinct formations from which innumerable plays are possible. Formation I illustrates a clockwise Two-Three revolving principle, which may be utilized anticlockwise if desired.

Play 1

Player 1 passes to 2 and drives around the outside to start the wheel. Wing player 2 breaks out to the ball and may pass to 1 or 4 cutting around him, or to pivot player 3. Player 3 meets the pass and sets up a blocking post. Pivot player 3 can either pivot back and shoot, drive to the basket, or pass off to 1. Players 4 and 5 revolve as shown in the diagram.

Play 1A

Player 1 starts the play and it develops as it did in regular Play 1. However, instead of the post player 3 passing off to 1, he fakes the pass and gives the ball to the second man around—in this case, 4.

Play 2

Player 1 again initiates the play, passing to 2 and wheeling, as shown. Player 4 follows 1. When 1 and 4 are under way, and just after 2 passes to 3, 5 breaks to a blocking position behind the opponent of 2. Player 2 starts to the left, reverses direction and drives to the right of 5's block and receives a return pass from 3.

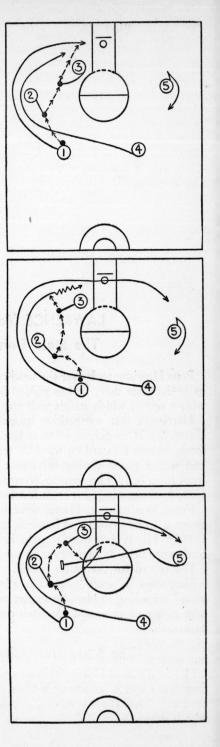

Play 2A

Player 1 passes to 2 and followed by 4, wheels as in the previous plays. The play develops as it did in regular Play 2, 2 passing to 3, 5 establishing a block behind 2's opponent. Player 2 cuts as in Play 2. Player 5 waits for his guard to attempt a switch to stop 2, then he (5) drives to his right and receives the ball from 3.

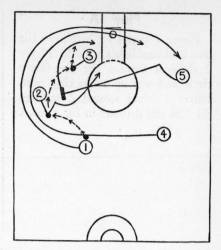

Formation II is the conventional Three-Two with three men working the ball in the back court and men posted in each corner for blocking and follow-in purposes. The area near the basket is kept open. This formation, as Harrison uses it, lends itself to both man-ahead-of-the-ball and ball-ahead-of-the-man maneuvers.

The man-ahead-of-the-ball plays involve backcourt screening designed to free a player who can drive into the uncongested area near the basket and then receive a pass from a backcourt teammate.

The ball-ahead-of-the-man attack involves a pass from a backcourt operator to one of the corner pivot or post men who break out to meet the ball. Thereafter, single and double screens are developed to free one of the backcourt players who can utilize a long cut from the backcourt to the basket area to outrun his opponent.

FORMATION II

Play 1

Player 1 passes to 2 who breaks out to meet the ball. Players 1 and 3 then follow the ball and establish a double block between 2 and the basket. Player 2 dribbles around the double block and moves in to the basket for the score.

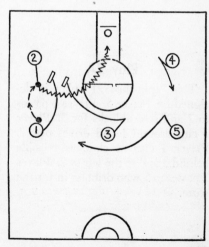

Play 1A

Player 1 passes to 2, follows the pass and establishes a block. Player 2 dribbles toward the free-throw circle and sets up a blocking post. Player 3 drives around 2, receives the ball and dribbles in for a score.

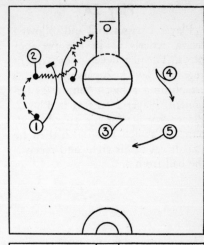

Play 2

Player 1 passes to 2 and moves to the left setting up a screenblock for 3. Player 3 drives hard around 1 and cuts by 2. Player 2 passes to 3, who dribbles in for the shot.

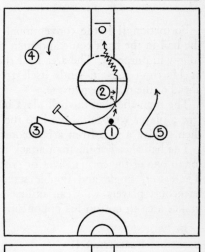

Play 2A

This "split-the-post" play is designed for Player 5. Player 1 passes to 2 and screenblocks for 3. Player 3 cuts around 1 and drives past 2. Player 5 cuts as close as possible behind 3 and to the left of 2. Player 2 passes to 5 who dribbles in for the score.

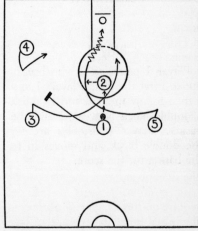

EDGAR S. HICKEY
St. Louis University

Teacher, lawyer, basketball chief, Eddie Hickey has been coaching basketball for twenty-two years. An outstanding athlete at Creighton University, Hickey graduated with a Bachelor of Laws degree, cum laude, and turned his talents toward coaching basketball.

After an eminently successful career as director of athletics and head coach of all sports at Creighton Preparatory School, Hickey went to Creighton University as head football coach in 1934. In 1935 he took over the basketball duties. Between then and 1943, when he entered the service, his teams won or shared in four conference titles, went twice to the National Invitation Tournament and took the consolation title at the western play-offs of the N.C.A.A. tourney one season. It was under his direction that the Creighton five broke the strangle hold the Oklahoma Aggies had on the Missouri Valley Conference title.

When Hickey entered the service and became a lieutenant commander in the Navy, the Aggies resumed their winning ways. The St. Louis Billikens displaced the Oklahoma five in 1946 with a record showing only one defeat—by the Creighton Bluejays—coached by Eddie Hickey.

In 1947, after his discharge from the service, Hickey was appointed head basketball coach at St. Louis University. His first season he rolled up a 21-3 record—and won the championship at the National Invitation Tournament.

Hickey's proudest accomplishment is the fact that during his entire collegiate coaching career only one member of his basketball squads has failed to finish his education and depart with sheepskin in hand.

St. Louis University's Offense

Eddie Hickey's St. Louis Billikens feature a Two-Three attack in Formation I. There is an overloading to both the right and left sides in the same formation. The center operates from a moving post or pivot within the free-throw area. A strong side forward is approximately five feet from the sideline and end line. The opposition forward is more "loose" from the basic position. Guards or "feeders" start most patterns which, at times, require an interchange of all positions except for the center. On some plays the initial move develops from the forward position.

Play 1

The guard goes around with an outside screen to free the original "feeder." Also, an outside screen by the center is designed to open up a second pass. Either "feeder" may initiate the play by interchanging positions in advance of the forward's move to meet the first pass. Players 5 and 3 rebound after scoring effort by 2. Players 4 and 1 take positions for defensive balance.

Play 1A

When the second pass to 3 is not open, 4, after feinting a pass to 3, turns to the outside and passes to 2 driving to the goal. Players 5 and 3 rebound along with 2. Players 4 and 1 take positions for defensive balance.

Play 2

Player 4 feints inside and receives a pass from 2. Players 1 and 2 delay timing and set double screen for 3. Player 5 passes to 3, who takes advantage of the screen. Players 2, 3 and 5 rebound 3's scoring effort. Players 4 and 1 take positions for defensive balance.

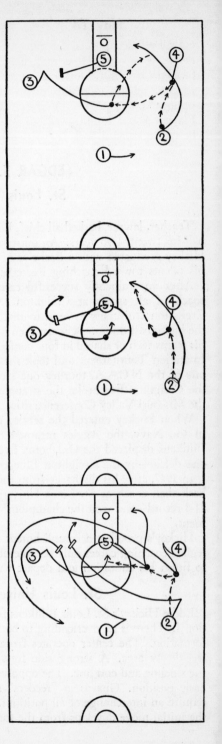

Play 2A

Player 5 sets post and 3 rubs off defensive coverage that may have broken through double screen. Player 5 may give or keep for pivot options. Players 2, 5 and 3 rebound. Players 4 and 1 take positions for defensive balance.

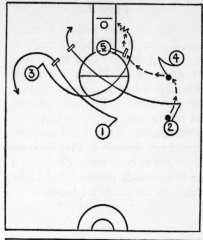

Play 3

Player 2 passes to 4 and cuts to goal (no screen) and out for safety. Player 4 passes to 5 on post and crosses to make running screen for 1. Player 5 hands off to 1, who makes scoring effort. Players 4, 5 and 1 rebound. Players 2 and 3 take positions for defensive balance.

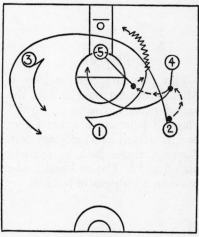

Play 3A

Should 5's guard switch to stop the scoring effort by 1, player 1 widens with dribble and passes to 5 who returns to goal. Players 4, 5 and 1 rebound. Players 2 and 3 take positions for defensive balance.

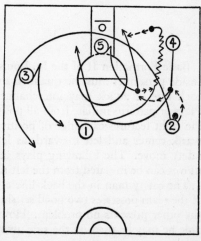

Play 4

Center (5) and 4 move to meet initial pass. As the pass is made to 4, player 5 clears keyhole by moving to strong side. Player 3 controls defensive guard and moves to post for pass from 4. Player 4 rubs out on post where 3 gives or keeps for pivot options. After initial pass and feint to go through as Play 1, player 2 returns to backcourt. Players 4, 3 and 5 rebound. Players 1 and 2 take positions for defensive balance.

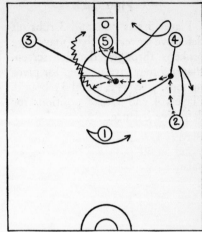

Play 4A

This play progresses as Play 4. After 4 rubs out on 3 at post, the second man, 5, crosses on "post." Player 3 passes to 5 either before or after rub out for 5's scoring effort. Player 4 circles back to rebound with 5 and 3. Players 1 and 2 take positions for defensive balance.

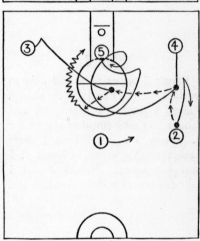

Basic Formation II of the St. Louis team features the Three-Two attack. Inside personnel must be qualified to operate from the post or pivot. The back line of attack may interchange personnel by figure eight or weave. Plays or patterns initiate from all positions in the back line. The attack from the right features exchange of positions between the right guard, right forward, center and left forward, as left guard controls defensive man in a safety move. The following plays show attack from the right side. Same moves can be initiated from the left side.

The safety man in the back line of attack should possess a good set shot. If the team possesses two good set shots, shifting the attack from one side to the other presents no problem. However, if but one good set shot is available he may be used on the side away from the attack.

Play 1

The center meets a pass from 2. Player 2 follows the pass for a running screen for 3. Center passes to 3 for dribble or scoring effort. Players 4, 3 and 2 rebound. Players 1 and 5 take positions for defensive balance.

Play 1A

This play has the same execution as Play 1. Then the center has option of handing off to 2 who initiates the play. Players 4, 3 and 2 rebound the scoring effort by 2. Players 1 and 5 take positions for defensive balance.

Play 2

The center meets pass from 2. In advance of initial move, forward 4 controls defensive man to baseline. Player 5 holds up pass from 2 until 3 has set screen for 4. Player 4 takes advantage of screen, receives pass from 5 for scoring effort. Players 3, 4 and 5 rebound scoring attempt. Players 1 and 2 take positions for defensive balance.

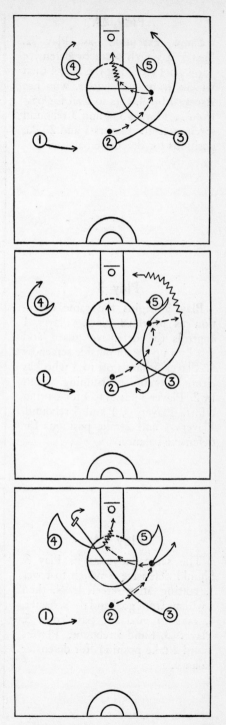

Play 2A

Same execution as Play 2. Should a switch occur by defensive 3 to stop 4 receiving the ball, 4 then widens from goal and 3, who has screened for 4, cuts to goal for pass from 5. Players 3, 4 and 5 rebound scoring effort. Players 1 and 2 take positions for defensive balance.

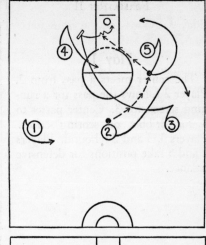

Play 3

Play 3 begins the same execution as previous plays. Player 1 controls the defensive guard and sets him up for an outside screen by 4. Player 5 hands off to 3 who has cleared because of running screen by 2. Player 3 passes to 1 for scoring effort. Players 3, 1 and 5 rebound. Players 4 and 2 take positions for defensive balance.

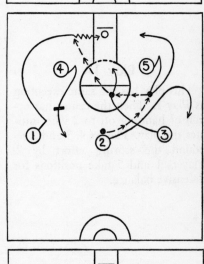

Play 3A

The same move as in Play 3. Should defensive 4 switch to cover 1, cutting after screen by 4, then 1 widens from goal and the screener, 4, cuts to goal for pass from 3. Players 3, 4 and 5 rebound. Players 1 and 2 take positions for defensive balance.

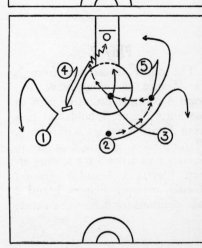

Play 4

Play 4 follows the previous pattern. Double screen by 4 and 3 as 1 maneuvers defensive man into position and then breaks to goal for pass from 5. Players 4, 1 and 5 rebound. Players 3 and 2 take positions for defensive balance.

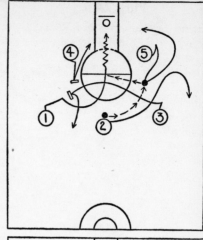

Play 4A

Play begins as Play 4. Player 5 hands off to 2 who advances with dribble. Players 4 and 3 set outside screen for 1. Player 1 cuts for goal to receive pass from 2. Players 4, 1 and 2 rebound. Players 3 and 5 take positions for defensive balance.

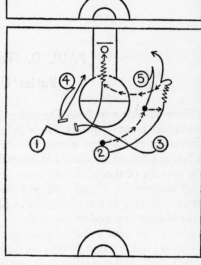

PAUL D. (Tony) HINKLE
Butler University

Tony Hinkle was born December 19, 1899, in Logansport, Indiana. He graduated from Calumet High School, Chicago, and then went to the University of Chicago where he received his Bachelor of Science degree. While at Chicago he starred in baseball, basketball, football, and soccer. He was captain of the basketball team in his junior and senior years. On the football team he played end and was a teammate of Fritz Crisler, now athletic director of the University of Michigan. In baseball, Tony held positions at shortstop and in the outfield. He also pitched at various times. He is one of two men to have earned nine letters from Chicago University.

Coach Hinkle came directly to Butler from the University of Chicago in March, 1921, and served under several athletic directors until 1934 when he was made director of athletics and head football coach. During the seven years ending with the 1941 season he coached the Bulldogs to seven Indiana Intercollegiate Conference football titles.

Hinkle was assistant basketball coach under Pat Page when the Bulldogs won their first national basketball title. In 1929, when they won seventeen of their nineteen games for a second national crown, Hinkle was head coach. In 1927, '28, '29, and '39, Butler won Indiana Intercollegiate Conference basketball championships. In 1933 and again in 1934, his squads swept to Missouri Valley titles. Tony also serves as Bulldog baseball coach.

During World War II, Hinkle served in the Navy, first as athletic officer at the U. S. Naval Training School, Great Lakes, and later as recreation and welfare officer on Guam. He was released from active duty with the rank of lieutenant commander. Tony has always been active in the National Basketball Coaches Association and has held numerous offices in that organization.

66

Butler University's Offense

Hinkle's Butler University five employs two styles of attack: (1) Stationary pivot man style and (2) Roving pivot man style.

Stationary Pivot Play

The two forwards and two guards pass the ball and move in a semicircle with inside and outside screens until the ball is thrown in to the pivot man. Then 1 breaks for the basket and continues to opposite side of the court. Player 2 circles to the left in front of 3 and 4. Player 3 cuts around 2 for the basket. Player 4 moves out around 2 for set shot. Options on this play: The Pivot Man (No. 5)

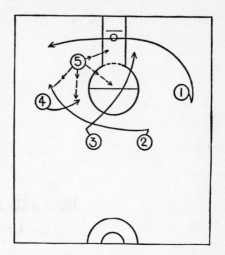

1. Passes to 1, if open
2. Passes to 3, if open
3. Passes to 4, for set shot
4. Pivots and shoots
5. Passes back to 2 or 4, and play starts over again.

Roving Pivot Play

Player 2 has the ball and passes to 1, moving toward the ball. Player 2 runs around 1; 1 fakes 2 the ball. Player 5 moves up and then away from the ball. Player 4 cuts around 5 and receives a pass from 1. Player 1 follows his pass. Player 3 cuts around 1. Options on this play: Player 4

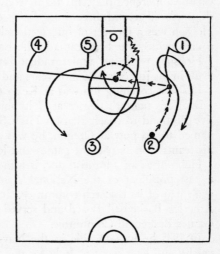

1. Feeds player 1, going into the basket
2. Feeds player 3, going into the basket
3. Turns and shoots
4. Passes back to 2 or 5, who have returned to backcourt.

HOWARD HOBSON
Yale University

Howard Hobson is one of the leading exponents of fast-breaking, hard-driving and high-scoring basketball. He has achieved an enviable record of coaching success. In eleven years at the University of Oregon, teams coached by Hobson won a total of 205 games, losing only 117. In Pacific Coast Conference play, his team won four Northern Division championships, placed second three times, finished third twice and fourth three times. Hobson was a pioneer of intersectional basketball and brought his Oregon squad to meet the best teams in the East at Madison Square Garden.

Hobson, while an undergraduate at Oregon, captained the basketball team in his junior and senior years and the baseball team in his senior year.

His first coaching job was at Kelso (Wash.) High School, and after receiving his master's degree at Columbia University, he returned to his native Portland to coach Benson High School. For four years before being named to his post at Oregon, he was at Southern Oregon Normal where his teams won sixty-eight games and lost fifteen.

Hobson, as an administrator, is a member of the board of directors and a past president of the National Association of Basketball Coaches and chairman of its research committee. In 1942 he was a member of the All-America Basketball Board and served as a member of the 1948 Olympic Games Basketball Committee.

In 1945 he was an aide in the Naval V-12 program at Columbia University and later went to Italy for one year as a sports consultant with the U. S. Army Special Service Force.

Hobson is recognized as one of basketball's foremost teachers and authors. His book on basketball technique, *Basketball Illustrated,* has been accepted as one of the best publications of its kind.

Yale University's Attack
against the Man-to-Man Defense

When the defense is entirely organized and set, a basketball team, to be effective, must have definite methods of attack. The style employed will depend largely on the offensive material and the type of man-to-man defense employed by the opponents. Here are a few general pointers:

1. Against a tight man-to-man defense, attack down the center lane.
2. Against a loose man-to-man defense that drops off to cover the key area, attack on the outside and use set shots with strong rebounding.
3. Cutting and screening plays are effective against man-to-man defenses in general.
4. Pass away from the defense and go to meet all passes.
5. Do not stand still and hold the ball. Keep players and ball moving.
6. Run plays that set up the best offensive threats and run plays at defensive weaknesses.

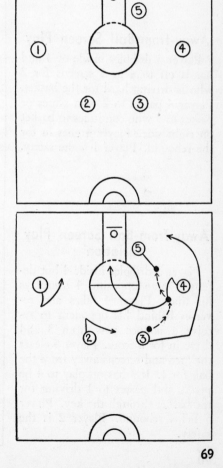

Basic Formation

Delayed Split Post Play

Player 3 passes to 4 and continues to sideline to occupy the defense. Player 4 passes to 5 and cuts close around 5. Player 4 may receive a return pass and drive in to basket. The usual pivot play options are possible. If 5 has no play with 4 he passes to 3 who drives hard on outside for score. Player 1 takes defense up court, then goes in for rebound. Player 2 is the safety.

Delayed Split Post Play Variation

Player 3 passes to 4 and cuts to sideline. Player 4 passes to 5 as 1 screens for 2 who is cutting hard for the basket on the outside. Player 5 passes to 2 for the score. Players 4 and 5 rebound. Players 3 and 1 are safety.

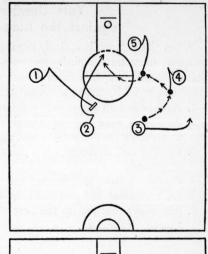

Away-from-Ball Screen Play

Player 3 dribbles inside of 4 and hands off to 4 as 5 screens for 2 who is driving hard for the basket. Player 4 passes to 2 who scores or passes to 3 who continues to basket on right side. Player 4 goes in for the rebound. Player 1 is the safety.

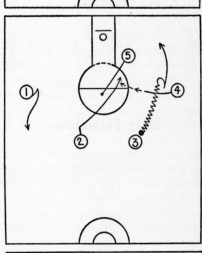

Away-from-Ball Screen Play Variation

Player 3 dribbles inside 4 but defensive man opposing 4 overplays his man. Player 4 fakes and reverses behind his opponent to receive a bounce pass from 3 and drive in for a score. Player 5 clears the area and screens away from the ball for 1. If 3 has no play to 4 he pivots and passes to 1 driving for the basket through the key. Player 5 helps rebound. Player 2 is the safety.

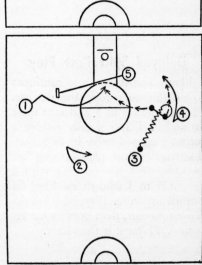

NAT HOLMAN
The College of the City of New York

Nat Holman has served more than thirty years as coach of the City College basketball team. Holman has been connected with the hoop game since his high school playing days. An all-around athlete, he won honors in scholastic basketball, baseball and soccer before trying the professional game with the original Celtics. Possessed of a fine set shot and exceptional speed, he captained and starred for the Celtics during the 1920's.

While playing as many as 120 games a season, Holman nevertheless found time to coach at City College and turn out some of the nation's leading teams. Beginning in 1917 as soccer and junior varsity basketball coach, he was promoted to head basketball coach in 1919, after a hitch in the Navy during World War I.

Holman-tutored teams are famous for their rapid short-passing, deft ball-handling and fast break attack. With teams composed of fast, small men, Holman has always stressed maintaining possession of the ball and working it in under the basket.

He was chosen coach of the East team in the annual East-West game at Madison Square Garden during the 1946-47 season. In the fall of 1946 he went to Mexico at the invitation of the National Federation of Basketball in that country to give lectures and demonstrations.

A former president of the National Association of Basketball Coaches, he was one of the first supporters of the move to eliminate the center tap. Many of his former pupils have become noted coaches and professional stars. Nat has had only two losing seasons at City College, and his lifetime record stands at 343 won and 120 lost.

The College of the City of New York's Offense

The offense used by Nat Holman's City College Beavers is based upon fast, short passes which are integrated into a number of formations. The shift from one formation to another is rapid because of the changing position of the pivot or post player.

Play 1

The pivot man (5) is between the endline and the free-throw line, while his other four teammates are spread out around the outer part of the front court. Player 1 takes a pass from 2, then throws an over-the-shoulder pass back to 2 who runs directly behind him. Player 1 then drives in, attempting to trap Defensive 1 into 5. As 1 slices across, 2 feeds a long lead pass to 1 who drives in for a shot. If 1 cannot make the shot, he will turn and feed off to 4 whose lane is momentarily cleared. Player 3 drives through and screens, thereby delaying Defensive 4, who is in pursuit of player 4. This play can be most effective if it has cadence and good timing. If the play is not successful, the ball is then thrown back and the men can proceed to attempt to go through this formation again. Either side of the floor can be used for the pivot man as the four outside men are spread around the outer area.

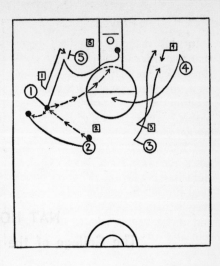

Play 2

This is a single post with a post man stationing himself on the foul line. Here again the four players, 1, 2, 3, and 4, are spread outside the foul line area. As No. 2 passes in to 5 he (2) immediately cuts through and simultaneously 3 slices off 5 who may take a pass and dribble in for the shot. As a pivot man, 5 keeps himself in readiness for the pass-off and if unable to pass to either 2 or 3, he can then feed off to 1 who comes in after 2 and 3 have sliced in. You will also note that 4 has dropped back as a safety player.

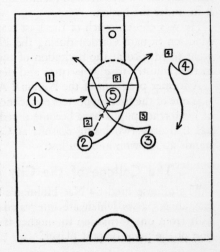

Play 3

In this diagram you will note that two men are playing back and three men are playing up. The big man, the pivot man (5) assumes a position directly underneath the basket. As 3 passes to 4, 1 cuts across and attempts to trap defensive 1 into 5. If he is successful, he takes the pass from 4 and drives right in for a lay-up. Player 1 must keep himself in readiness for whatever situation may present itself and if he cannot shoot, he must spin and turn ready to feed a teammate. Players 2 and 3 slice, hoping to delay their opponents as they drive in with them. If either one of these two get clear, 1 can feed the ball to them. He should also watch out for any other player who may break away from his opponent.

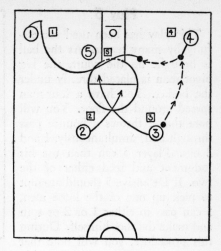

Play 4

Play 4 is somewhat of a variation of Play 3, but you will note that all four of the players, 1, 2, 3, and 4, are outside, while 5 is still in the pivot position directly underneath the basket. As the ball is brought up the court, 4 makes a long, two hand, over-the-head lead pass to 5. If the pass is successful, 3 screens across in front of 2. Player 2 fakes left just as 3 starts. As he goes across, and when he gets to a given point, 1 also slices off, and may trap Defensive 1. Now there are two opportunities for men to get clear and if they are successful, 5 can feed either one of the two as they drive in for the basket. You will also note that 4 pulls back toward the center of the court to serve as a safety man in the event that things go wrong.

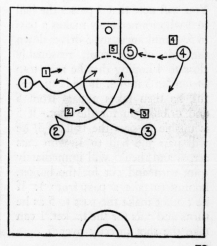

Play 5

This play has been used successfully by many teams. As the ball is brought up the court, the big pivot man is placed directly under the basket. You have a four-man spread around the floor. You will note that 2 throws a bounce pass through and, simultaneously, 1 and 2 cut. Player 5 can then use his judgment and feed either of the two. If Defensive 5 should attempt to pick up one of the loose men, 5 can pass to either 1 or 2 or spin and make the shot himself. During this procedure, you will note that 4 comes across from the other side of the floor to participate in the scoring. Player 5 knows this and keeps himself in readiness to feed off to three men who may be coming across on this particular play. Player 3 swings over into the center of the court to serve as safety.

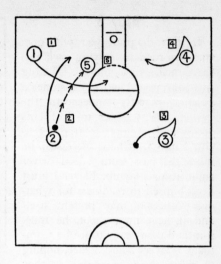

Play 6

Here three men spread out across the floor on a line even with the foul line. This play can be used on opponents who are not on the alert to cross-check the coming screens. You will note that 2 passes the ball to 4 who immediately makes a pass to 5. Simultaneously, 3 drives down the side of the court reasonably close to 4 hoping that he may trap Defensive 3 into 4. If he is successful, he then takes a pass from 5 and dribbles in for the shot. If 5 is unable to pass the ball to 3, he will pass the ball to 1, who cuts across and then 5 will immediately spin, turn and cut for the basket, hoping to take a pass from 1. If he cannot make the pass to 5 as he turns and cuts for the basket, 1 can take the shot directly over 5.

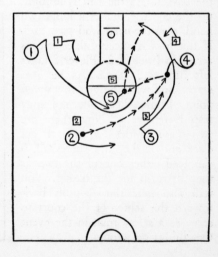

74

Play 7

Play 7 is a variation of Play 6. This time the screen goes on the inside instead of the outside. You will note that 3 passes the ball to 4, who immediately passes the ball across to 5. Player 3 then drives through the center between 4 and 5 and, at a given moment, 4 cuts across and takes the pass from 5 on the pivot position. Player 5 can feed 4, and if 4 cannot get through, 5 can feed off to 1. This is a very difficult play for the opponents to check as either 4 or 1 can definitely get a shot off from the foul line. Player 2 remains back as a safety should the play go badly.

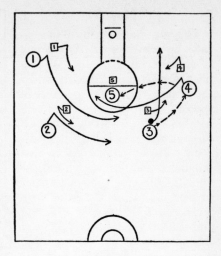

HENRY P. IBA
Oklahoma A. & M. College

"The most conservative coach in basketball," Henry Iba is one of four brothers, all former outstanding athletes in Missouri collegiate circles.

After three years at Westminster College, Iba began coaching at Classen High School, Oklahoma City. At Classen he began an eminently successful career (fifty-one games won to only five lost in two seasons) that led him to coaching positions at Maryville, Missouri, and the University of Colorado. In 1934, he completed a cycle, so to speak, by returning to Oklahoma where A. & M.'s basketball was in the doldrums.

The first impressive Aggie team came in 1936-37 when the Oklahoma five won twenty, lost three, and won the Missouri Valley pennant unchallenged. Subsequently, Iba coached the Aggies to eight full Missouri Valley conference championships and a share of three others. His teams have won sixteen conference or state championships during his twenty-two years of coaching. In addition, they have added two N.C.A.A. (1945 and 1946) championships to their list of basketball honors.

In addition to his basketball duties, he is director of athletics at A. & M. and prizes most the year 1945-46 when A. & M. won the Sugar Bowl championship in football, N.C.A.A. championships in wrestling and basketball, the National ROTC championship in rifling, and developed seven All-Americas in various sports.

Progressive in policy, soundly conservative in coaching methods, his teams each year have the best defensive record in the nation.

Oklahoma A. & M.'s Offense

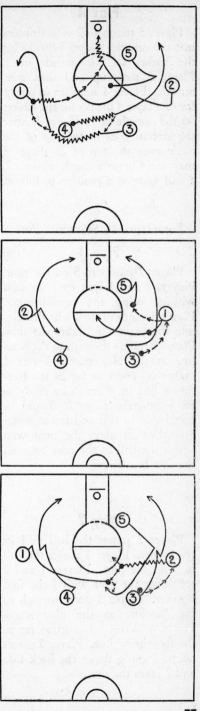

FORMATION I

Play 1

Player 4 dribbles and passes to 3. Player 4 screens for 2 with 5 helping on the screen. Player 3 dribbles and passes to 1 and continues on in to the corner. Player 1 dribbles and passes to 2 who is cutting over the middle off the screen. If 2 is not open, 1 may pass to 5 who comes back over the middle after screening for 2. Players 2, 5, and 4 follow on the backboard.

Play 2

Player 3 passes to 1. Player 1 passes to 5 on the post and steps inside toward the middle after the pass. Player 3 breaks for the basket going on the outside of 1. Player 2 steps inside toward the middle the same as 1 and 4 breaks for the basket going on the outside of 2. Player 5 may use 3 or 4, or may spin and shoot himself or he may pass to 1 who comes over the middle. Player 2 is ready to go back on the defense. Players 5, 4 and 3 are up for the rebound.

Play 3

Player 3 passes to 2 and goes inside 2 to screen. Player 2 dribbles into the middle. Player 4 goes inside to screen for 1 who comes over the top of 2. Player 2 may use 4 going to the basket or he may use 1 over the top. Player 5 steps up and then outside over the top of 1 which would mean a double exchange at the top of the circle. Players 3, 4 and 2 would be in a position to follow.

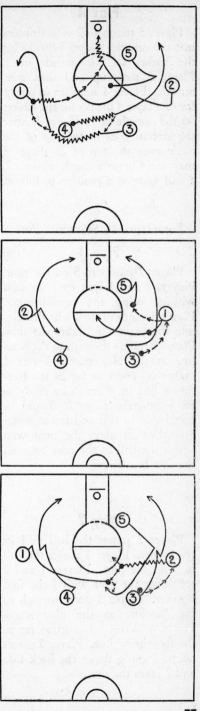

Play 4

Player 3 passes to 2 who dribbles into the middle. Player 3 breaks for the basket on the outside of 2. Player 5 steps up and then goes outside. Player 1 steps up to screen for 4. Player 4 breaks for the basket on the outside of 1. Player 1, after the screen, goes to the top of the circle over the top of 2. Player 2 may use 4 or may use 1. Players 2, 3 and 4 are in a position to follow.

FORMATION II. SPLIT THE POST

Play 1

Player 2 passes to 5 on the post. Players 2 and 1 split over the post with 2 being the first breaker. Player 5 hands off to 1 who dribbles into the basket and takes the shot. Player 3 moves through to the base-line as the play starts. Player 1 moves up court as far as the free-throw line in order to be ready to come into the play. It should be noted that in this and forthcoming Split-the-Post plays the man who passes the ball to the post becomes the first breaker.

Play 2

Player 2 passes the ball to 1 in the corner. Player 1 passes the ball to 5 on the post. Players 1 and 2 split over the post with 1 the first breaker. Player 3 goes through to the baseline as the play starts. Player 4 moves up court as far as the free-throw line. Player 5 passes off to 2 going down the back side and 2 takes the shot.

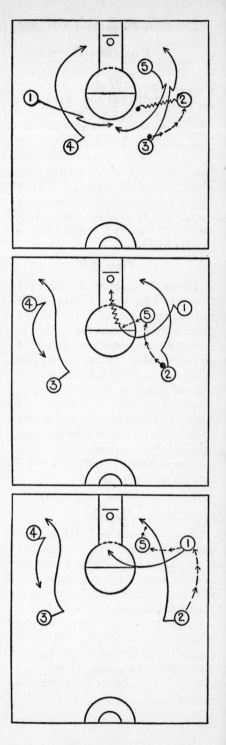

Play 3

Player 2 passes into the post to 5. Players 2 and 1 split over the post and 5 hands off to 1. Player 3 moves through to the baseline as the play starts. Player 4 moves up court as far as the free-throw line, suddenly reverses and cuts for the basket. Player 1 who has received the ball from 5 on the post takes one dribble and passes to 4 who is cutting for the basket.

Play 4

Player 2 passes to 5 on the post. Players 2 and 1 split over the post and 5 does not use either of them. Player 3 moves through to the base line and out to the corner as the play progresses. Player 4 moves up court as far as the free-throw line and as 5 misses both 2 and 1 he moves out to assume the same position on this side of the floor as 2 started on the opposite side. Player 5 dribbles and resets the post on the opposite side of the lane. Notice that 4, 3 and 5 now have the same set upon the left side of the floor as 2, 1 and 5 had on the right side. Player 5 has the ball on the post.

Play 4A

Player 5 had the ball on the post after resetting the post from the opposite side. He now passes the ball out to 4. Player 4 passes the ball to 3 in the corner. Player 3 passes back to 5 on the post. Players 3 and 4 split over the post with 3 as the first breaker. Player 5 hands the ball off to 4 coming down the back side and 4 takes the shot. Players 2 and 1 have moved out on the opposite side to assume their original positions.

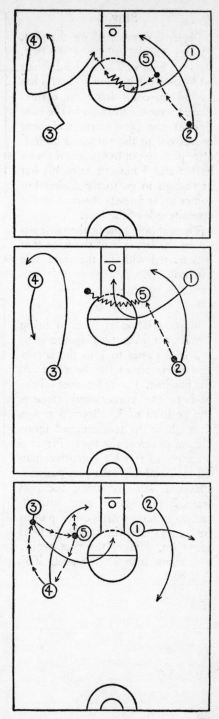

Play 5

Player 2 passes to 5 on the post. Players 2 and 1 split over the post. Player 5 hands off to 1 who dribbles and passes the ball out to 4 who has moved up court from the corner. Player 3 moves through to the base line as the play starts and now moves out to the corner. Player 1, after passing out to 4, goes on under basket and 5 now turns to his left as though to go to the basket but comes up and resets the post on the opposite side of the lane.

There should now be the same set-up on the left side of the floor that was started with on the right side—4 outside, 3 in the corner, and 5 on the post.

Play 6

This variation is used to bring a different man to play the post. Player 2 passes to 1 in the corner and starts across the floor toward the baseline. Player 5 moves off the post to the corner and assumes the position of 1. Player 3 moves through to the baseline and meets 2 coming across the floor. Player 3 attempts to rub his defensive man off on 2 and takes the post position. Player 1, after receiving the pass from 2, dribbles up court and attempts to hit 3 with a quick pass as he comes under the basket. If he is not open, 3 takes the post which brings about the original setup with a different man on the post. This post change can be done as often as desired.

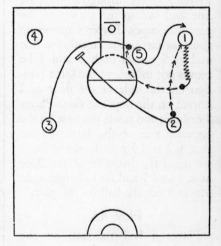

ALVIN (Doggie) JULIAN
Boston Celtics
Basketball Association of America

Doggie Julian first came over the sports horizon as a Bucknell Bison where he was an outstanding athlete, winning letters in football, basketball and baseball. After graduation he was signed by the International League Reading baseball team. Farmed out to York, of the New York-Pennsylvania League, he broke a finger and was forced to forego his active baseball career. He took up coaching baseball, and a year later became manager of the Chambersburg team of the old Blue Ridge League.

Then Julian entered the collegiate coaching profession and soon was leading Muhlenberg College to success on both the gridiron and the basketball hardcourt. During the nine years Julian was at Muhlenberg, his teams were consistently at the top of the Eastern Pennsylvania Conference. During the war years, Muhlenberg's personnel was bolstered with V-12 material and Julian came up with a splendid two-year record of forty-four wins and but nine defeats. Both years, the Mules participated in the National Invitation Tournament.

Julian coached at Holy Cross for three seasons, bringing to that institution national fame and honors in basketball. Now with the Boston Celtics in the National Basketball Association, Julian is proving to once-skeptical New Englanders that football, baseball, and ice hockey have a keen sports rival in basketball.

The Boston Celtics' Offense

The Boston Celtics' offense comprises the use of two basic formations. The first is known as the Middle Pivot. In this formation, the center is placed on the free-throw line with the two forwards playing directly on line with the center but near the sidelines. The forwards should be tall men, good shots from the side, and know the mechanics of cutting off of the pivot and screens. The two guards must be good passers, expert in feeding the post or pivot, and good screeners.

Play 1

Player 4 passes to 1, screens inside and goes almost to the baseline and comes back out. Player 1 passes to 3 and cuts around him. Player 5, timing himself with 1, cuts off 3 for the pass and the shot. Player 2 moves out to a defensive position.

Play 1A

This play operates just like Play 1 with the exception that player 1 cuts to the corner and screens for 2. Player 5 stays out. Player 5 can also screen for 2 if desired.

Play 2

Player 4 passes to 3 and goes over to screen for 5. Players 1 and 5 double cut off of 3. Player 2 stays out of the play. Player 1 cuts first.

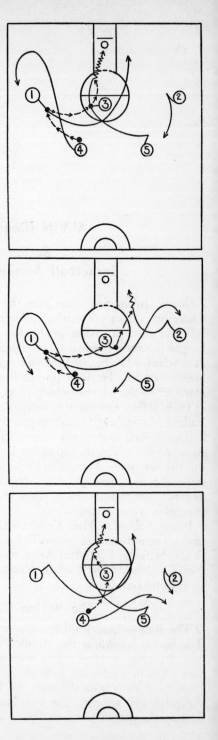

Play 2A

On this variation, 4 passes to 3, fakes a cut, pulls out and screens for 5. Player 5 cuts and receives pass after 1 has made his cut. This is a good play, in spite of its apparent simplicity.

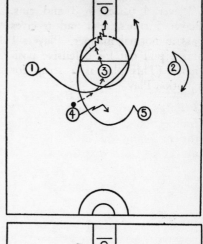

Play 3

In this outside screen play, 4 passes to 1 and runs outside. Player 1 passes to 3 and cuts off of him. Player 4 receives the pass from 3.

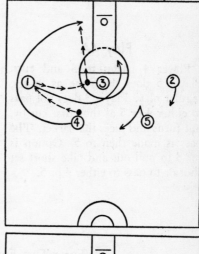

Play 3A

Player 4 passes to 1 and runs outside to the baseline and pulls out. Player 3 moves over to screen for 2 who receives pass from 1. Player 5 holds his position.

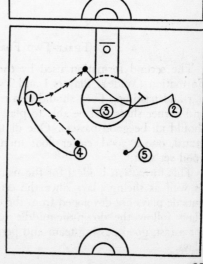

Play 4

Player 4 passes to 3 and cuts. Player 5 times, cuts and receives pass in normal manner. Players 1 and 2 pull out for defensive positions. (This play is a setup for variation Play 4A.)

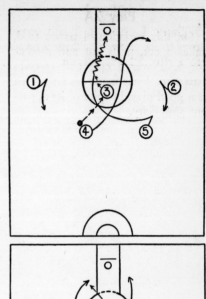

Play 4A

Player 4 passes to 3 and cuts. Player 5 does the same as in the regular play. Player 3 does not pass to either 4 or 5 as they first cut by, but turns and faces the basket. The pass is made then to 5. Option is for 3 to pull out and take short set shot or to pass to either 4 or 5.

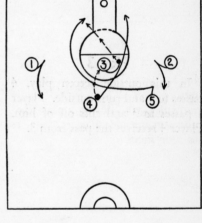

THREE-TWO FORMATION (WIDE)

The second formation used by the Celtics is the standard Three-Two Formation (Wide). Players 1 and 2 should be tall for advantage in receiving and passing. They should also excel at rebounding, possess good side and corner shots and be able to play the post or pivot. Players 3, 4 and 5 should all be good passers. One of these men should be a good rebound guard, one a good, clever floor man (playmaker), and one should be a good set shot.

This formation is ideal for the usual down-the-middle give-and-go plays as well as slicing plays since the center of the court is kept open. The outside plays are developed from the old guard-around type and the slicing plays follow the down-the-middle scissors style. The formation is ideal for a fast, good passing team and permits the development of many clever plays.

Play 1

Player 4 passes to 5 and comes over to screen for 3. Player 5 passes to 3 after 3 fakes outside.

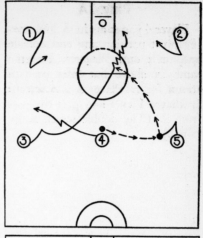

Play 1A

Player 4 passes to 5 and screens for 3. Player 3 fakes a cut and pulls out. Player 2 has moved into a moving pivot. Player 5 passes to 2 and cuts outside. Player 2 can pass to 5 or shoot.

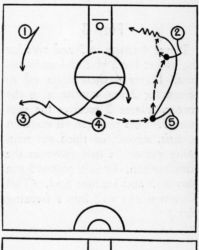

Play 2

Player 4 passes to 2 who has gone into a moving pivot. Player 4 cuts outside to the near baseline and pulls out. Player 5 times his cut off 4's defensive man and receives the ball from 2. Player 5 should fake outside and come across as diagrammed.

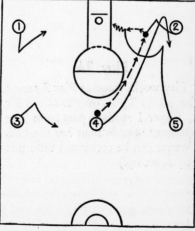

Play 2A

Player 4 passes again to 2 in moving pivot position and cuts outside and pulls out. Player 5 does the same as above but goes over to screen for 1. Player 3 also screens 1. Player 1 cuts and gets the pass from 2. (The double screen is optional.)

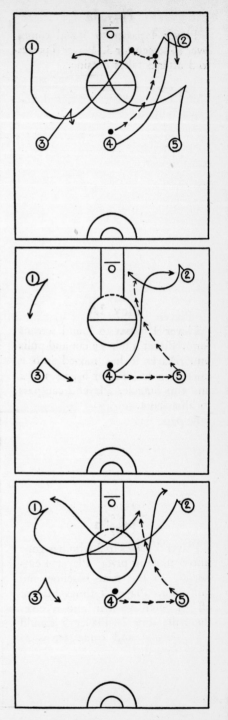

Play 3

Player 4 passes to 5 and cuts for the basket for a give-and-go return pass. Player 4 then slides off to screen for 2 and continues to the corner. Player 2 receives the pass from 5. This play can be executed to first, second, or third cut man using player 4's first move as the basic pattern. In fact, player 5 can pass to 3 and let him feed. (This pattern works well into a freezing play.)

Play 3A

Play works same as Play 3 except that player 2 goes over to screen for 1. Player 1 receives pass from 5 or whatever outside man has the ball. (Weave can be continued until this play is set up.)

Play 4

Player 4 dribbles into moving pivot. Player 1 cuts off him and toward the basket. Player 3 times his outside cut to break closely behind 1. This forces a quick double-switch by the defense.

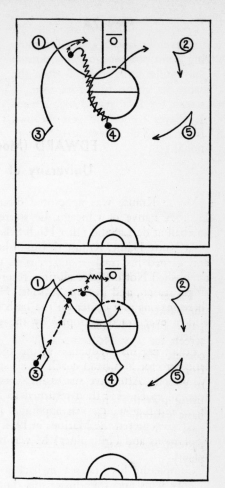

Play 4A

Player 1 moves into a sliding pivot spot. Player 4 goes in and sets up beside him. Both men have their backs to the basket. Player 3 passes to 1. Player 1 hands the ball to 4 and cuts around him. Player 3 then cuts outside 4 and receives the pass.

EDWARD (Moose) KRAUSE
University of Notre Dame

Moose Krause was appointed director of athletics at Notre Dame in 1949. A native of Chicago, he starred in football, basketball, track and baseball at de LaSalle (Ill.) High School.

At Notre Dame, Krause distinguished himself in football and basketball, and earned his track monogram in the javelin throw. In basketball, he established Notre Dame all-time records for scoring in a single game, in a single season, and in three seasons. He was an All-America in each of his three seasons as a center on the Irish quintet and is the only Notre Dame athlete ever voted a trophy by the student body for his prowess as an athlete.

Following his graduation at the age of twenty-one, Krause became athletic director and head coach of all sports at St. Mary's College, Winona, Minnesota. After five successful years, he went to Holy Cross as assistant football coach. He then returned to Notre Dame in a similar capacity in 1942, and that winter was appointed head basketball coach.

Krause entered the Marines in 1944. After fourteen months in the Pacific (Solomons and Philippines) he was discharged with the rank of first lieutenant.

Completing his first season back as a basketball coach with a record of twenty wins and four losses, his quintet was victorious over most of the nation's best teams. Since then, Krause has consistently produced expertly coached teams well versed in the principles he learned under the late George Keogan who was one of basketball's greatest tutors.

The Notre Dame Pivot Offense

Ed Krause's Irish quintet uses the pivot attack almost exclusively. Ed was an All-America center (pivot player) for three successive years as an undergraduate and his own prowess as a ball handler and scorer is undoubtedly responsible for Notre Dame's success in the use of the pivot attack. A brief study of the plays which Krause has developed from the Two-Two-One and Two-Three player alignments reveals the importance he places in the pivot operator. It is important to keep in mind that the pivot player can, and is expected to, turn and try for the goal himself in addition to passing off for teammates. The pivot man's shots usually follow a fake pass to cutting teammates.

Play 1

Player 1 passes to 2 and cuts around the outside. Player 2 passes to 3 and drives across-court in front of 3. Pivot player 3 passes to 1 for the shot and pivots away from the pass for a return pass or to follow the shot. Players 4 and 5 set up the defensive balance.

Play 2

Player 1 passes to 2 and cuts around the outside. Player 2 passes to the pivot player (3) and cuts across to the outside. Player 3 passes 2 the ball for the shot and pivots away from the pass for a return pass or to secure a good position to follow in. Players 4 and 5 again retreat to set up the defensive balance.

Play 3

Player 1 dribbles to the right and passes the ball to the pivot player (3). Player 1 then cuts to the right and around 3. Player 2 fakes to the right, reverses and charges closely behind 1 and to the left of 3 on the free-throw line. Player 3 can pass to either 1 or 2. Players 4 and 5 set up the defensive balance.

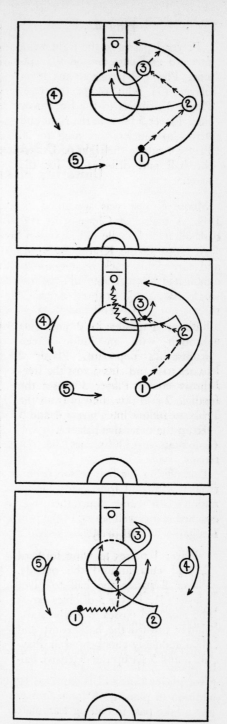

Play 4

Player 1 passes to the right wing forward and cuts around the outside. Player 2 passes to the pivot player (3) who meets the pass. Player 3 dribbles to the free-throw line. Player 5 fakes to the right and drives to the left screening for 4. Player 4 cuts to the right of 3, takes the ball and dribbles in for the score.

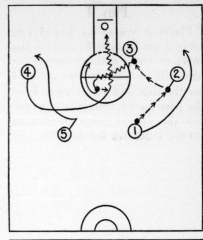

Play 5

Player 1 passes to 2 and cuts through with an inside screen against 2's opponent. Player 2 passes to 3 and cuts across the free-throw circle. Player 3 passes the ball to 2 and pivots away from the pass to follow in. Players 4 and 5 set up the defensive balance.

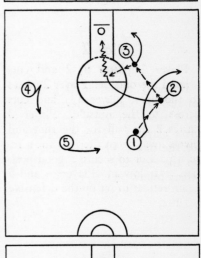

Play 6

Player 1 passes to wing forward 2, and cuts around the outside. Player 2 passes the ball to pivot player (3). Player 3 dribbles across the lane and passes to 4 who starts slowly toward the back court and then suddenly cuts behind 3. Players 2 and 5 set up the defensive balance.

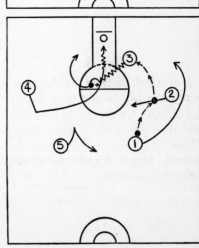

Play 7

Player 1 passes to 2 and cuts to the outside and clear around the court. Player 4 follows around behind 1. Player 2 meets the ball and passes to 3. Player 3 passes to 4 for the shot and pivots the opposite direction for the follow in. Players 1 and 5 set up the defensive balance.

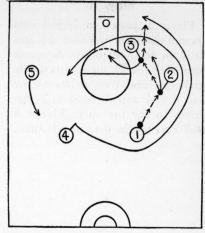

Play 8

Player 1 passes to 2 and cuts around the outside. Player 2 passes to 4 who has been screened by pivot player 3. Player 4 dribbles in for the score. Players 5 and 2 set up the defensive balance and the others follow in.

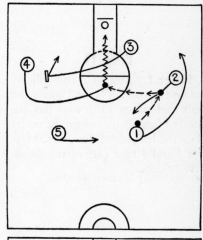

Play 9

Player 1 passes to 2 and cuts to the outside. Player 2 meets the ball and then passes to 3 on the post. Player 3 passes to 1 cutting on around. Players 4 and 5 set up the defensive balance.

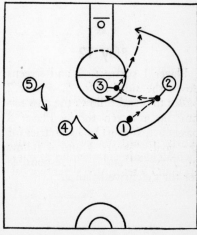

Play 10

Player 1 passes to 2 and cuts around the outside. Player 2 passes to 3 on the post and cuts across after the pass. Player 4 starts slowly backcourt and then drives to the left of 3. Player 3 passes to 2 who drives in for the shot. Players 5 and 3 set up the defensive balance.

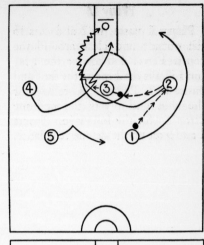

Play 11

Player 1 passes to 2 and follows around outside. Player 2 meets the ball and passes to 3 who has cut around behind the screen set up by 5 on the left side of the court. Players 2 and 4 take care of the defensive balance.

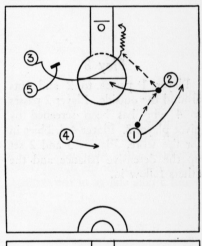

Play 12

Player 1 passes to 2 and screens down the sideline for 5. Player 2 passes to 3 and follows the pass setting up a screen for 3. Player 3 passes across-court to 5 who tries for the goal. Players 3 and 4 follow in. Players 1 and 2 are responsible for the defensive balance.

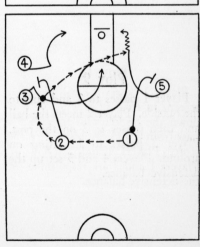

Play 13

Player 1 passes the ball to 2 and follows for an outside screen. Player 2 passes to 3 cutting for the goal and follows the pass across the free-throw line. Player 4 follows 2 closely and takes a back pass from 3 for a good shot. Players 1 and 5 are responsible for the defense.

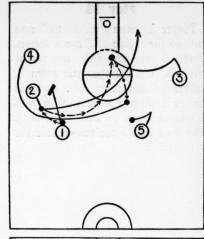

Play 14

Player 1 passes to 2 and cuts around the outside. Player 2 meets the pass and dribbles across to the free-throw circle. Player 3 fakes to the left and drives behind 2 at the free-throw circle and takes the ball and dribbles in for the shot. Players 4 and 5 take charge of the defense.

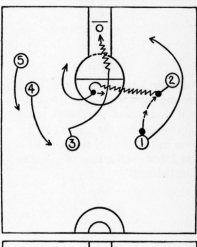

Play 15

Player 1 passes the ball to 2 and screens in front of 3. Player 3 cuts down the middle and receives the pass from 2 and dribbles in for the score. Players 4 and 5 follow in. Players 1 and 2 are responsible for the defensive balance.

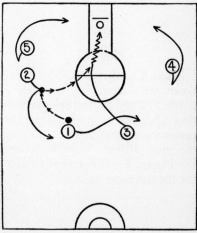

Play 16

Player 1 passes the ball to 2 and cuts to the inside of 2 for a screen. Player 3 cuts across the free-throw circle and takes the ball from 2. Player 4 follows 3 closely. Player 3 pivots if stopped and passes back to 4 who dribbles on in for the shot. Players 1 and 5 are responsible for the defense.

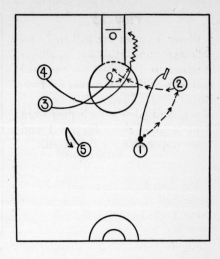

JOSEPH LAPCHICK
New York Knickerbockers
Basketball Association of America

Joe Lapchick, mentor of the New York Knickerbockers, has been a basketball name for a quarter of a century. Born and raised in Yonkers, New York, Lapchick learned his basketball with neighborhood teams and launched his professional career with the Hollywood Inn Five, a semi-pro team in Yonkers. Then came jobs with Holyoke, Schenectady and the Brooklyn Visitations before he joined the Celtics in 1922.

Lapchick remained with the Celtics until 1927 when the old American League was disbanded. Along with Dutch Dehnert and Pete Barry, Celtic teammates, he moved to the Cleveland Rosenblooms. He helped the Rosenblooms win two league titles, then went to Toledo for one year as player-manager. In 1930, he reorganized the Celtics and they toured the country until 1936 when Lapchick accepted the coaching post at St. John's University, Brooklyn, New York, ending a career of eleven successful seasons with basketball's most famous professional team.

Lapchick left St. John's in 1947 to coach the New York Knickerbockers. During the eleven years he coached at St. John's, four of his teams were the New York Metropolitan District champions and seven qualified for the National Invitation Tournament. Two of these teams (1943 and 1944) were tournament champions.

Joe's teams are clever and reflect sound teaching in their technique and tactics. As you would expect, Joe specializes in the pivot and post attack because he spent many years as one of the top professional performers in the pivot and post positions. The plays and formations used by the Knickerbockers call for ball-ahead-of-the-man principles coupled with good backcourt screening and clever ball handling by the frontcourt pivot or post player.

The New York Knickerbockers' Offense

The Knickerbockers quick-break at every opportunity. Sports fans like action and the fastest pace in basketball is found in quick-break tactics. If the quick break fails to materialize, the Knickerbockers set up a pivot man near or under the basket and attempt to score by means of that player's pivot and turn shots. Failing that, Formation I offense, which calls for the pivot man to move to a post position on the free-throw line, is employed and the set formation plays are attempted. Formation II calls for a double post attack.

Play 1

On the single cut off the post player, player 3 passes to 4. Simultaneously, player 1 feints right and then moves behind 2's opponent. Player 2 then feints left and cuts to the right of the post and receives a hand-off from 4. Player 2 then dribbles in to the basket. Players 1, 5, and 3 are responsible for backcourt protection.

Play 2

This post play is a variation of Play 1. It involves a double screen. After player 1 sets up a backcourt screen for 2, 2 passes to 5 and cuts to the right of the post. There, he reverses his field and cuts back behind 4 where he may attempt a down-the-middle set shot or cut to the left and dribble in to the basket.

Play 3

Player 2 passes to 5 who meets the ball. Player 1 fakes to the right and then sets a screen behind 2's opponent. Player 2 fakes left and cuts to the right of the post. Player 5 passes to 4 who gives ball to 2 as 2 cuts by. Player 4 then pivots in opposite direction from pass and drives toward basket. Player 2 can dribble and pass back to 4 if 4's opponent has switched to cover him.

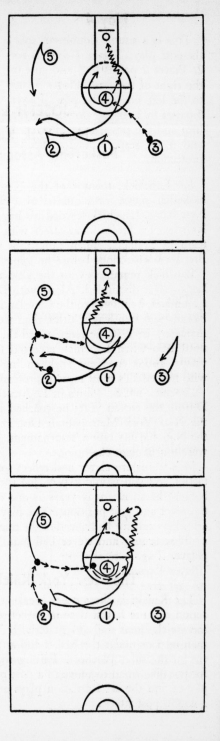

Play 4

This is a simple double-cut split-the-post play. Player 1 screens for 2. Player 2 passes to 5 and cuts to the right of the post. Player 3 cuts to the left side of the post. Player 5 passes to 3 cutting down between him and the post player. Players 1 and 4 are responsible for defense protection.

BASIC FORMATION II

Play 1

This is a down-the-middle play for 3 in a double post formation. Player 1 passes to 5 after 2 has screened between 1 and his opponent. Player 2 continues on over and also screens inside for 3. Player 3 breaks closely behind 2's inside screen and drives down the center of the court and receives the pass from 5. Players 4 and 5 pivot to the outside and follow in.

Play 2

This is an alternate for Play 1. Player 2 again screens for 1 and 3. Player 1 passes to 5. If 3 is unable to get free from his opponent, 5 fakes the ball to 3 but holds it until post player 4 has had time to cut across the lane and set up a block behind 5's opponent. Then, 5 drives in for the shot. Players 1 and 2 are responsible for the defense.

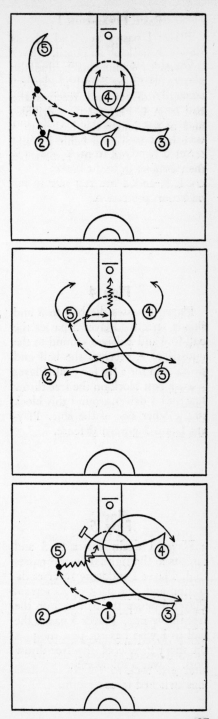

Play 3

Player 1 passes to 3 and screens slowly in back of 3's guard. Player 3 passes to 4 and cuts behind the screens set up by 2 and 5. Player 1 suddenly drives and receives the ball from 4. Player 1 then dribbles and passes under the basket to 3 who has cut around behind 2 and 5. Players 2 and 4 are responsible for the defense.

Play 4

Player 1 passes the ball to 3 and slowly screens. Player 3 passes the ball to 4 and 2 drives around to the outside of 4, receives the ball and dribbles in for a try for goal. Player 5 sets a post block on the free-throw line and 3 drives around this block to the other side of the lane. Players 1 and 5 govern defense.

Play 5

Player 1 again passes to 3 and screens to the right. Player 3 passes to 4. Player 1 suddenly reverses direction and cuts back of 2's screen. Player 4 passes the ball to 5 on the free-throw line. Player 5 passes the ball to 1 who has cut past the post on the left side of the free-throw post. Player 5 follows in.

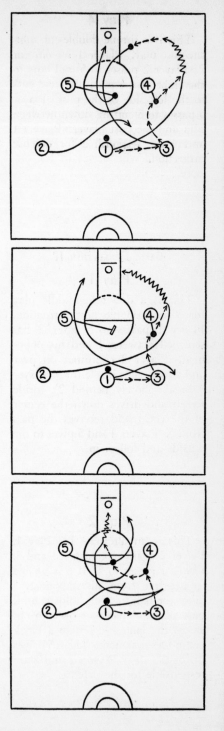

Play 6

Player 1 passes ball to 3 and screens slowly to the right. Player 3 passes the ball to 4. Post Player 5 moves to the free-throw line and takes the pass from 4. Player 2 moves slowly to the right and then puts on speed and cuts behind 1's screen and to the left of 5. Player 5 passes to 2 who drives in for the score.

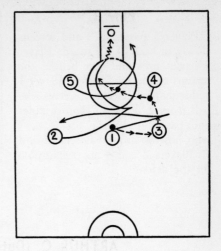

ARTHUR C. (Dutch) LONBORG
Northwestern University

Coach Arthur Lonborg, dean of Big Ten basketball coaches, began coaching at Northwestern University in 1927 after a brief but successful career at McPherson and Washburn Colleges in Kansas. During his 22-year coaching tenure at Northwestern, Lonborg's teams have been consistently successful, winning two Western Conference championships and finishing out of the first division only six times. The Wildcats were conference title holders in 1931 and in 1933.

Lonborg graduated from the University of Kansas in 1921 where he was all-Conference in basketball, football, and baseball.

After leaving Kansas, he became athletic director and basketball coach at McPherson College where in two years his teams won twenty-three games and lost four. He went to Washburn College at Topeka, Kansas, in 1924, where in four years he won two conference championships and a national A.A.U. championship. While at Washburn his teams won forty-nine games and lost nine.

Coach Lonborg is an exponent of the short-pass offense as contrasted with the fast break. His system is based upon thorough individual grooming of players who fit into a well-developed offense based upon a series of definite plays.

While at Northwestern, Lonborg has produced a number of outstanding players, including Joe Reiff, conference scoring champion in 1931 and 1933; Max Morris, scoring leader in 1945 and 1946, and Otto Graham, who won All-America honors in 1943. In addition to coaching basketball, Lonborg is also assistant football coach.

Northwestern University's Offense

Coach Lonborg uses two formations in his Northwestern University offense, the Three-Two and the Two-Three. Although Lonborg's teams can

100

use the quick break when opportunity presents, they are better geared to regular team play which employs short passes and a well-defined pattern of play. Dutch coaches what is known as "position basketball" where players are individually groomed to fit into certain positions with definite duties in the completion of the set plays.

In the Three-Two formation, three players expert in the handling of the ball operate between the free-throw circle and the ten-second line. Two frontcourt pivot or post men work out of the corners usually handling the ball under the ball-ahead-of-the-man principle.

In the Two-Three formation, two backcourt passers and cutters usually start the plays with a pass forward and then employ screens and long cuts to drive in for a score. The three frontcourt men usually assume positions on a line which extends across the court in the vicinity of the free-throw line or in line with the junction of the lane and circle.

Three-Two Formation Plays

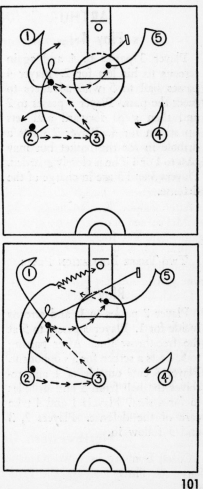

Play 1

Player 2 passes to 3 and cuts down the left sideline. Player 3 passes to 1 who breaks out to the pass. Player 2 screens for 1 and goes on over and sets up a screen for 5. Player 1 may shoot or pass to 5 for a shot. Players 3 and 4 are responsible for the defensive balance. Players 1, 2 and 5 follow in after the shot.

Play 2

Player 2 passes to 3, and again screens for 1 and 5. Player 3 passes to post player 1 and cuts around the outside. Player 1 passes to 5 who passes back to 3 for the shot. Players 1 and 4 are responsible for the defense. Players 2, 3 and 5 follow in after the shot.

Play 3

Player 3 passes to 4 and moves to his left to screen for 2. Player 2 cuts hard for the basket behind 3's screen. Player 4 may pass the ball to 2 or 5 coming out toward him. If 4 passes to 5, 5 can relay the ball to the cutter (2). Players 3 and 4 are responsible for the defensive balance.

Play 4

Player 3 passes to 4 and again screens to his left for 2. Player 4 passes ball to 5 who advances to meet the pass. Player 5 passes to 2 and then steps forward and sets up screen for 4. Player 2 starts a dribble in for the basket but may pass to 1 or 4 if he is closely guarded. Players 3 and 5 are in charge of the defense.

Two-Three Formation Plays

Play 1

Player 2 passes to 1, and screens inside for 1. Player 1 passes to 5 at the free-throw line. After passing to 5, 1 sets a screen for 3's opponent. Player 3 cuts outside of 1 and receives the ball from 5 and dribbles in for a shot. Players 1 and 4 take care of the defense. Players 2, 3 and 5 follow in.

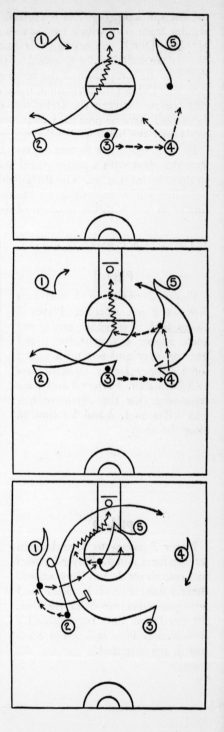

Play 2

Player 2 passes to 1 and screens across to his right for 3. Player 1 passes to post player 5, and again sets a screen for 3. Post Player 5 passes to 3 for the shot. Players 1, 3 and 5 follow in. Players 2 and 4 are responsible for the defensive balance.

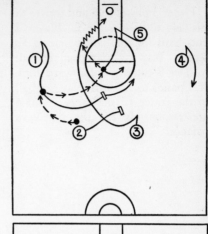

Play 3

Player 2 passes to 3 and screens 3's opponent. Player 3 passes to 5 and cuts around teammate 2 to the left. After 3 has started his cut, 2 splits the post to the right. Player 5 may pass off to the free man or attempt a shot himself. Players 1 and 4 are responsible for the defense.

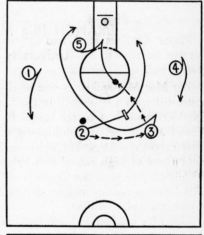

Play 4

Player 2 passes to 3 and screens 3's opponent. Player 3 passes to 5 and cuts to the left to screen for 1. After 3 has cut, 2 continues on and sets up a screen for 4. Player 5, on the free-throw line, may pass to 1 or 4 or dribble or shoot. Players 2 and 3 are responsible for the defense.

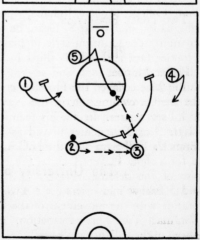

BRANCH (Big Mac) McCRACKEN

University of Indiana

Big Mac McCracken is one of the old school coaches who first got acquainted with a basketball in the family barnyard, throwing a stuffed hog bladder through a barrel hoop. Big Mac is a typical Hoosier, his slow drawl and homespun philosophy making him a favorite speaker at Indiana sport meetings. Hailing from Monrovia, Indiana, McCracken played four years of high school ball before entering the University of Indiana. While playing with the Cream and Crimson squads, he won Big Ten and All-America ratings and set a new individual scoring record in Western Conference play in 1930.

Upon his graduation from Indiana, Mac took the coach's position at Ball State College, Muncie, Indiana, where he stayed for eight years. Upon the resignation of Everett S. Dean, he took over at Bloomington. Completely changing the Crimson style of play, he introduced the fast break style to Hoosier fans and led his third Indiana University team to the N.C.A.A. championship.

Big Mac coached the Hoosiers continuously from 1938 to 1943 and then accepted a commission in the Navy, serving until the beginning of the 1946-1947 season. In all, his teams have won approximately 70 per cent of the Big Ten games played as well as capturing six runner-up titles. Branch's 1940 team won the N.C.A.A. title.

The University of Indiana's Offense

McCracken's Hoosiers use a Two-Two-One formation which changes in outline with the movement of the Pivot-Post player from the basic formation to a Two-Three formation. All of the plays incorporate the man-ahead-of-the-ball principle.

Two-Two-One Formation Moving into Two-Three Formation

Play 1

Player 1 passes the ball to 2 and screens across behind 2's opponent. Player 2 dribbles closely behind 1 and then passes the ball to post player 3 who breaks to the pass. Player 4 sets up a screen in front of the circle and 1 drives hard around him and toward the basket. Player 3 passes the ball to 1 for the shot. Players 4 and 5 are back for defense.

Play 2

Player 1 again passes to 2 and screens across for 2 and 4. Player 2 again dribbles in and passes to post player 3. Player 4 cuts behind 1's screen, around in front of 3 on the post and receives the ball and dribbles in for the shot. Players 1 and 5 are back for defense.

Play 3

Player 1 passes to 2 and slowly moves to the right. Player 2 passes the ball to 4 who breaks to the pass. Player 4 passes to 3 and screens slowly in front of the free-throw circle. Player 1 suddenly sprints for the basket behind 4's screen and receives the ball from 3 for the dribble and the shot. Players 2 and 5 are back for defense.

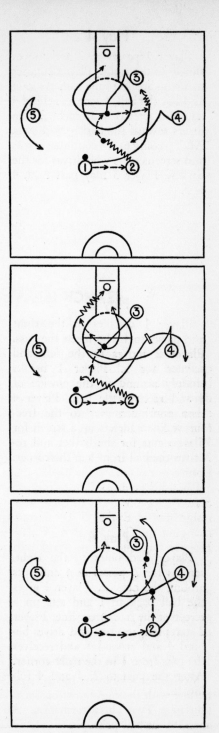

Play 4

Player 1 passes to 2 and moves slowly to the right. Player 2 passes to 4 who breaks to the ball. As soon as 4 has the ball, 1 screens behind 4 and also screens in front of 2 who drives toward the basket as shown. After passing to 3, 4 continues across and screens for 5 who drives for the basket. Player 3 may pass to 2, 4 or 5.

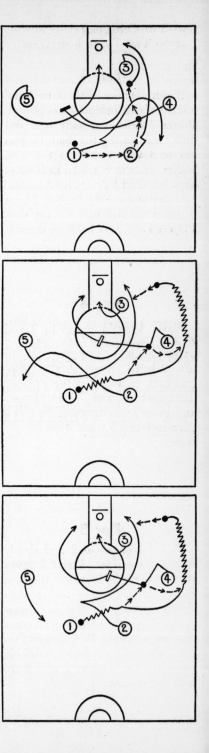

Play 5

Player 1 dribbles to the right and passes to 4 who meets the pass. Player 2 moves to the left and screens for 5. Player 1 breaks sharply around to the outside of 4 and receives the ball. Player 4 then continues over to the free-throw line and sets up a screen for 5 who cuts for the basket and receives the ball from 1 in the corner.

Play 6

Player 1 dribbles to the right, screens for 2, passes to 4 and cuts around the outside. Player 4 gives the ball back to 1 and sets up a screen at the free-throw line. Player 2 starts left, reverses and drives behind 4 and around 3 and receives the pass from 1 in the right corner. After the pass to 2, 3 and 4 follow in.

Play 7

Player 1 passes to 2, starts right and reverses to the left behind a screen set up by 5. Player 2 passes to 3 who breaks to the free-throw line. Player 2 then starts to his left, changes direction suddenly, and drives around the outside of 4 who has screened for his drive to the basket. Players 4 and 5 again come back for defense.

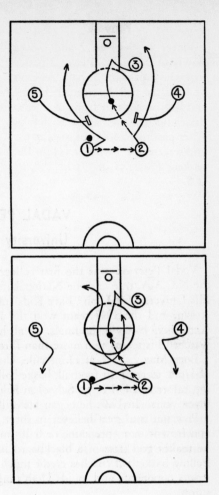

Play 8

Player 1 passes to 2 and screens to the right behind 2. Player 2 passes to 3 and starts slowly to his left. When 1 reverses direction and cuts back to the other side of 3 on the free-throw line, 2 also reverses and joins 1 in "splitting-the-post." Players 4 and 5 come back for defense.

VADAL PETERSON
University of Utah

Vadal Peterson was the first college coach to have his teams win both the N.C.A.A. title and the National Invitation Tournament championship. His University of Utah "Blitz Kids" of 1944 walked off with the N.C.A.A. crown, and the 1947 team won the Invitation Tournament by downing Kentucky, 49-45, in the finals. In all his years of coaching at Utah, he has watched his teams win more than three-fourths of their games.

Born May 2, 1892, at Huntsville, Utah, Peterson attended the University of Utah, starring in football, basketball, and baseball. He began his coaching career at LDS High School in Salt Lake City in 1920, remaining there seven years. In 1927, he began his brilliant career at Utah.

Peterson is a great believer in short, well-planned daily practice sessions, and frowns upon pre-game or half-time oratory in the dressing room. But he makes good use of a blackboard both before a game and at half-time. Fellow basketball coaches credit much of Peterson's success to the way he scouts opponents and molds Utah's offense and defense to meet the opposition.

Vadal's teams are prepared to vary their basic offensive pattern seven different ways. His teams follow a fluid offensive system in working the ball from the center of the floor toward the basket. The Single Post system is used. On defense, Peterson teaches a strict man-to-man system. Players are given definite defensive assignments before the game starts, and these can be changed only on orders from the bench.

The University of Utah's Offense

The best way to combat a good man-to-man defense is by good ball handling and split-second timing plays with every man carrying out his offensive assignment perfectly. Utah's basic formation starts out in a Two-One-Two alignment and then shifts rapidly depending upon the movements of the post player. Peterson believes that the post man should be constantly on the move, stopping for his part in the plays at a spot just outside the free-throw circle.

Play 1

Player 5 passes to the post, starts to the right and reverses down the middle. Player 4 breaks with 5 and, with proper timing, one of them, usually 5, will lose his guard long enough to be free for a pass from 1. Players 2 and 3 move out to the spots left vacant by 4 and 5.

Play 1A

The only variation in this play is for the post man (1) to pivot and shoot or dribble using one of the cutters as a screen in case 4 and 5 are not free.

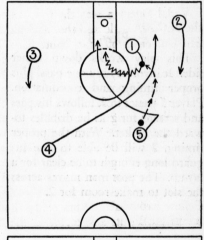

Play 2

In this play, 4 passes to 5. Player 4 then follows his pass, making it possible for 5 to use him as a screen. Player 5 drives down court in to the basket, using 4 as a screen. Player 1 moves out of the slot with his guard to give 5 a clear path into the basket.

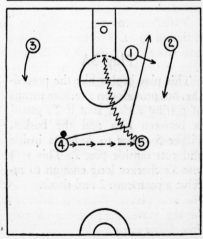

Play 2A

This play is most effective against a sliding defense. Player 4 passes to 5 and cuts as shown. If player 4's opponent slides to cover 5, it will leave 4 free for a return pass from 5. The post man pulls out to the right, clearing a path for 4 to drive toward the basket.

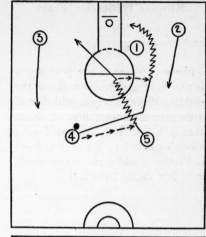

Play 3

This play works down either side. It involves only one pass, plus proper timing and coordination. Player 5 passes to 2, follows his pass and screens for 2 as he dribbles toward the basket. With the proper timing, 2 will be able to lose his guard long enough to be clear for a lay-up. The post man moves across the slot to make room for 2.

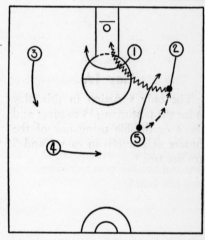

Play 3A

This play begins like the preceding, but provides an alternate means of getting a clear shot if 2's guard is between him and the basket. Player 5 passes to 2, feints inside and cuts outside past 2. This will lose 5's checker long enough to receive a pass from 2 and shoot.

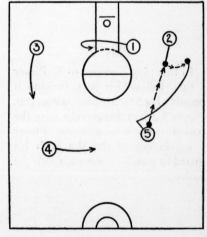

Play 4

This play begins like Play 3A, but involves more finesse. If properly executed, it can become a very successful play. Player 5 passes to 2 and screens 2's opponent. Player 2 passes in to the post and cuts by 1 for a return pass. Proper execution gives 2 a shot at the basket.

Play 4A

This play is almost identical to the foregoing, except that it allows for the probability that 5 will not be able to screen 2's guard. In this event, 2 will not pass to the post. Instead, he dribbles toward the basket and uses the post man for screening his guard.

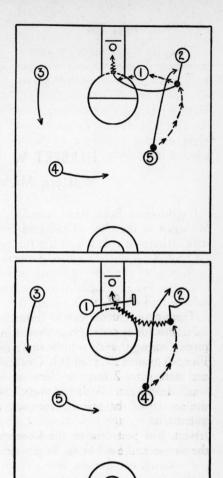

HERBERT W. (Buck) READ
Western Michigan College

English-born Buck Read completed his basketball coaching at Western Michigan at the close of the 1948-1949 college year in accordance with a state retirement rule which sets the age limit at seventy.

Coach Read has always sought perfection in his work, involving finger-tip control of the ball, fast wrist action, speed on the floor and the ability to dig up loose balls and intercept passes. He advocates the conversion of defense into offense with a rush, trying to secure a scoring position before the opposition defense can be formed.

Perhaps his success is best shown in the record of the past twenty-seven years. During that time his teams have played a total of 498 contests, winning 340 against a loss of 158. Of these twenty-seven teams only three have lost more games than they have won, and one of them was undefeated. Read's teams ran a string of forty-nine straight home games, lacking just one contest of making it a complete five-year period without a defeat in Kalamazoo.

Buck was president of the Coaches' Association in 1948-1949. He has always worked hard in the organization, serving as chairman of the rules and research committees, and also as secretary-treasurer. A keen student of the game, he has advanced a great number of ideas for the betterment of basketball which has been literally his life's work.

Western Michigan College's Offense

The attack on a defense that has become set follows two general principles: working with the pivot circle open and with the pivot circle closed. The offense which follows will combine the two types of play and add a principle of rotation. Read works with the pivot circle open as the basic formation and uses pivot play around the basket only as a secondary formation.

The basic formation is the Two-in and the Three-out. It places the center in the right corner; the tallest forward in the left corner, the fastest forward and ball-hounder at the right outcourt spot; the best feeder, headiest player, and best outcourt shot in the center; and at the left side, a third player who is a sort of all-around man. He can fill in the feeder's spot, shoot well from outcourt, go in and play a pivot occasionally and be made the captain of "emergency" defense.

Play 1. Basic Rotation

Player 4 with the ball starts the figure eight pattern by passing to 2 and cutting to the corner occupied by 3. Player 2 passes to 5 and cuts to the opposite corner. Player 3 comes up to get the ball from 5, and ultimately passes to 1. This is mechanical but sets the pattern for the offensive plays to follow.

Play 2. Reverse Rotation

Player 4 passes to 5 and goes to the left corner. Player 5, instead of coming across court with a dribble or a pass, pivots back to the sideline and passes to 1. Player 5 then pivots back and cuts toward the basket. Player 2, ostensibly coming across to take a pass from 5, pivots back and cuts down the right sideline behind 3's screen. Player 1 may pass to 5 or to 2.

Play 3. Backcourt Screen

Player 4 starts the play by passing to 2, reversing and screening behind 5's opponent. Player 5 starts down the left sideline and then cuts behind 4's screen and drives for the basket. Player 2 may pass directly to 5 or pass to 3 in the corner. If the pass is made to 3, he must meet the ball and then relay it to 5.

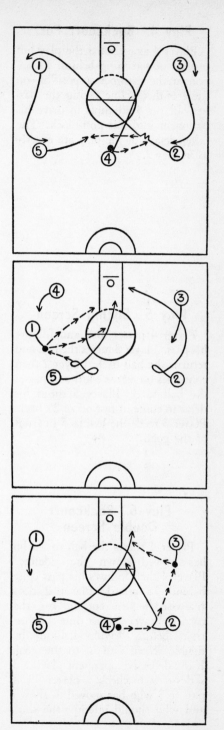

Play 4. Backcourt Post

Player 4 again starts the play but instead of screening behind 5's opponent, he assumes a position on the free-throw line facing the basket. Player 5 attempts to drive his opponent into this post-block. The other details of the play are exactly as in Play 2.

Play 5. Slicing Screen

Player 4 passes to 2 and follows his pass. Player 2 meets the ball and returns the ball to 4. Player 2 then continues on across court as 4 passes the ball to 3. Player 5 times his drive to come in fast off of 2's back. Player 3 feeds the ball to 5 in front of the goal.

Play 6. Backcourt Double Screen

Player 4 passes the ball to 5 who has moved down the sideline. Player 4 then follows his pass close behind 5's guard. Player 2 does likewise, before cutting for the corner. Player 5 must time this just right before driving behind the double screen and in to the goal. If the defensive opponent playing 3 slides over to check 5, player 5 can pass to 3 who has moved as shown and who should attempt the shot.

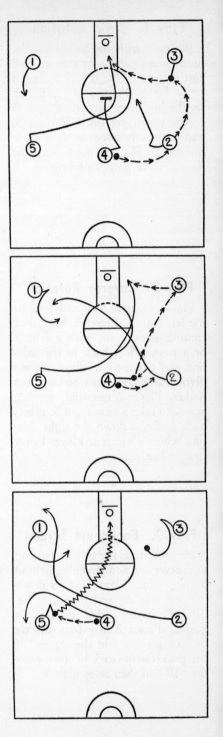

Because the center is not tall enough for consistent pivot work the area in front of the basket is kept open. However, we may wish to use a pivot and the formation which follows will work effectively.

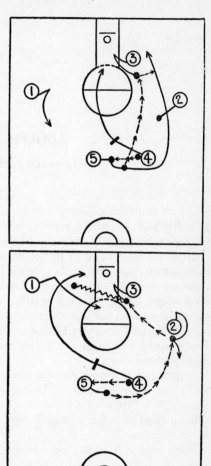

Play 7. Pivot

Player 4 passes to 5 and screens behind 5's opponent. Player 5 steps forward and pegs the ball to 3. Player 3 pivots for the shot or passes off to 4 who has slid his block, or to 5 who has gone around 2.

Play 8. Pivot Dribble Screen

Player 4 starts the play by passing to 5 and screening behind 5's opponent. Player 5 fires a pass to 2 on the right sideline. Player 2 passes to 3 on the pivot. Player 3 fakes a shot and dribbles to the left side of the lane, where he is split by 1 and 4. Player 3 may shoot or pass to 1 or 4.

ADOLPH F. RUPP
University of Kentucky

The "Baron of Basketball," Adolph Rupp, proved his title when the Wildcats from the University of Kentucky won the 1948 N.C.A.A. championship and shared the right to represent the United States in the 1948 Olympics in England with the Phillips "66" Oilers.

Since the Baron's reign in the South began in 1930, the Wildcats have been beaten only eight times on their home floor, and have now won sixty-three straight tilts on the Alumni Gym hardwood. They have won twenty-six straight tilts in a period overlapping two seasons, and over a five-year period, have won forty-five straight conference encounters.

In 1944, the Baron was elected to basketball's Hall of Fame, the highest honor in the basketball world. He was the tenth coach so honored in the history of the sport.

A native of Halstead, Kansas, where he captained his high school basketball team, Rupp went to the University of Kansas where he played under Phog Allen. After his graduation from Kansas (1923), he coached for one year in high school at Marshalltown, Iowa, and then at Freeport, Illinois, for four years.

Rupp spends his spare time farming in the Blue Grass region of Kentucky.

University of Kentucky's Offense

The Kentucky offense is one of pressure. The Wildcats will take advantage of every opportunity to quick-break but even when the quick-break opportunity is not present, the Rupp-coached Wildcats hustle the ball into offensive territory and give the opposition little time to relax. The set attack is built around a post player who usually works from the free-throw line. However, when Rupp comes up with a good pivot scorer (Edwards, Groza) he employs this man near the basket to take advantage of his shooting ability. The basic formations are the Two-Three and the Three-Two with the frontcourt men working out of the corners.

Play 1

Player 1 passes to 2 who comes out to meet the pass. Player 2 flips the ball to 1 as 1 cuts by. Player 1 dribbles, pivots and passes in to 3 on the post. Player 2 has reversed by this time and screens for 1 who cuts around 2 and the post player (3) as shown. The ball is passed to the open player.

Play 2

The same ball handling takes place in this play as in Play 1. However, in this case, player 1 screens for 2 after he passes to the post player (3). Again 3 passes to the man who succeeds in breaking away from his guard.

Play 3

Player 1 passes to 2. Player 2 passes to the post player (3). Player 1 cuts in as if to get the ball. In fact he may get it. But, in this case, 2, after passing to 3, sets a block screen on the opponent of 5. Player 3 passes to 5 or to 2 depending upon which one succeeds in getting free from his opponent.

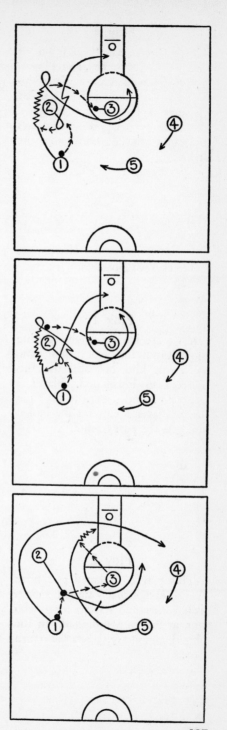

Play 4

The fundamental execution of this play is the same as in Play 3. There is a tendency for the defensive man guarding player 1 to let up after 1 fails to get the pass. When this occurs, post man 3 passes to 1 right after 1 passes under the basket.

Three-Two Formation Plays

Play 1

If we are having trouble getting the ball in to the pivot or post man, we move him out and use this Three-Two Formation. Player 1 passes to 2 and screens to his right for 5. Player 5 cuts for the basket and gets the pass from 2.

Play 2

This play is executed exactly as Play 1, except that 5 starts his cut a little earlier and screens for 1 who cuts in the path indicated. In the play shown above, 1 gets the return pass.

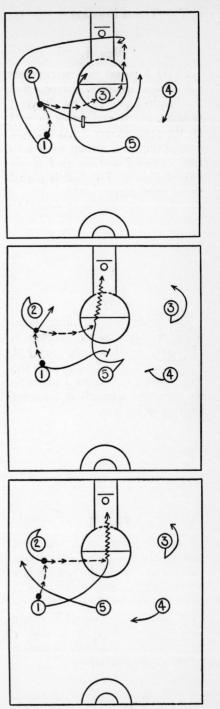

Play 3

Player 2 starts the play by passing to 1. As 2 passes he starts toward the basket and swings back to screen for 3. Player 1 passes to 4 who breaks out to meet the pass. Player 4 passes to 3 who is cutting down the middle of the floor.

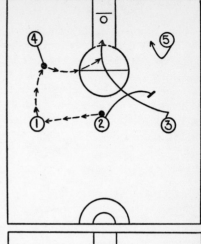

Play 4

Player 1 passes to 2 and cuts diagonally across the free-throw circle. Player 2 passes to 4 who comes out to meet the pass. As in all plays, the man who does not have the ball must do the timing on the play. Player 3 cuts behind 1 and receives the ball from 4.

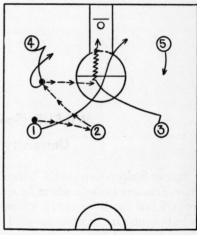

WILBUR (Sparky) STALCUP
University of Missouri

Sparky Stalcup came to the University of Missouri from Maryville (Mo.) State Teachers College where he was head basketball and track coach and football line coach for eleven seasons—1933 to 1942 and in 1945. At Maryville, Stalcup's teams never finished out of the first division in the Missouri Intercollegiate Athletic Association. They were represented in six N.A.I.B. tournaments in Kansas City during his tenure, and were runners-up for the N.A.I.B. tourney title in 1943.

As a player, Stalcup learned his basketball under Henry Iba—then basketball coach at Maryville. He was an all-sports participant earning eleven major letters at Maryville—three in football, and four each in basketball and track. He captained the track team, and was all-conference selection in basketball and football. His greatest honor, however, came in 1932 when he was named a second team All-America guard after competing in the National A.A.U. basketball tournament.

Stalcup was born at Forbes, Missouri, on February 10, 1910. His basketball career was launched at Oregon High School, Oregon, Missouri. There he captained the state championship team, and was selected as an all-State forward. Upon his graduation from Maryville Teachers in 1932 (B.S. Degree), Stalcup coached all sports at Jackson (Mo.) High School for the 1932-33 season. His Jackson team was runner-up for the state title.

University of Missouri's Offense

BASIC FORMATION

The ball can go to player 5, the post, from either 3 or 1. As shown, 3 passes to 5. Both 3 and 1 break around 5, 3 breaking first. This procedure at times is reversed with 1 breaking first followed by 3. In either instance, a natural screen is formed. If 5 does not elect to give the ball to 1 or 3, then 4, the third breaker, drives by the post. Player 2 moves out slowly as the play develops to the positions originally occupied by 4 and then on to the original player 3 position. (If a shot is taken over the top by 3 or 4, then 1, 2 and 5 are the rebounders with the shooter following to the head of the free-throw circle.)

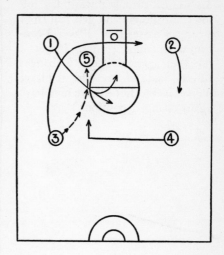

THE CHANGING POST

Play 1

All men are taught to play the Post or Pivot position. This figure shows the movement of players in changing the Post.

Player 3 passes the ball to either 5 or 1. After passing, he breaks in front of 5 and forms a screen for 2. Player 1 dribbles out toward the center line looking first for 2. If screen set by 3 has been effective, 1 gives ball to 2 for a shot. If not, he dribbles out and can pass back to 5 or 2 who now occupies the post position. Player 5 moves into the position vacated by 1.

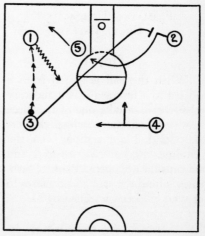

Play 2

Player 3 dribbles toward 4. As 3 starts his dribble toward 4, 1 follows him slowly and gets ball from 4 after 3 passes to 4. Player 3 continues to right corner. Player 2 takes left corner. Player 5 changes to other side of lane just as player 4 gives ball to 1. (All five men have again changed positions.)

Play 3

Occasionally we move 5 to the free-throw line and have 3 and 4 scissor over the top. Player 5 can pass to either depending upon which is free. Players 1 and 2 move out to positions vacated by 3 and 4.

Play 1

When the ball is passed from a guard to a forward it is mandatory that the man take one of the three positions on the baseline. Players 1, 5 and 2 are stationed on the endline. Player 4 passes to 2 and screens his opponent. Player 2 dribbles behind the screen and passes to 1 who has been screened by 5.

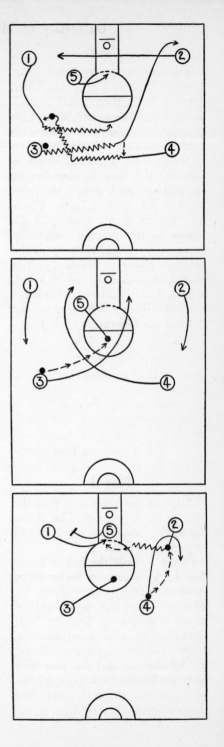

Play 2

Double Screen. Player 3 passes to 1 and follows path of ball, cutting inside of 1. As ball is passed, 4 and 5 screen for 2. Player 2 comes over the top for a pass from 1.

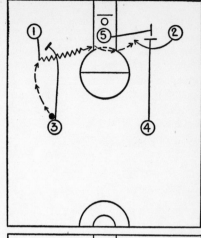

Play 3

Player 4 passes to 2 and screens for 5. Player 5 comes out for a pass from 2. If close enough and clear, he shoots. If 5 cannot shoot, he sets up a post and 2 and 3 criss-cross in front of the post—both looking for the ball and the shot.

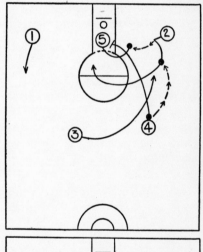

Play 4

Player 3 dribbles toward 4 and passes off to him. Player 3 then continues and screens for 2 at the baseline. Player 4 dribbles and passes to 1 who is coming out to meet the ball. Player 4 continues on to the baseline and 5 screens for 4 (delayed). Player 1 passes to 2 or to 4 who cuts back to the basket.

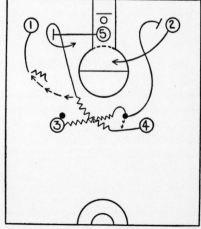

Part II

ATTACKING THE ZONE DEFENSE

THE ZONE DEFENSE

Many basketball enthusiasts have contended for years that continued use of the zone defense would ruin spectator interest in the game. Time has not supported their position. Undoubtedly the most determined effort to ban the zone defense from basketball is the rule which is enforced in the Basketball Association of America. This league, the largest and most important of the professional leagues, penalizes a team which uses this type of defense by forfeiture of the game. Yet, "sagging" or "floating" tactics are employed perforce by every team in the league.

Despite the bitter attacks which have been made against the use of the zone defenses in basketball, the fact remains that zone defenses are still used by approximately 80 per cent of all high school teams and about 20 per cent of all colleges. The editor of this book contends that every defense employs the principles of the zone. Most of the college teams stressing "exclusive" use of the man-to-man defense, "sag" or "float" whenever their opponents maneuver the ball near the basket or to one side of the court.

Where does the man-to-man "sagging" or "floating" defense end, and where does the zone begin? What is the definition of that part of the man-to-man defense which occurs, in effect, whenever the ball enters scoring territory and the defending players drop back under the basket? Can it be said that such "sagging" or "floating" conforms to man-to-man principles?

What happens when a ball goes up in the air for a shot? Most defensive teams zone the rebound area, disregarding their assigned opponents completely, in an attempt to station their players so that one of them will be in whatever area the ball may fall. Is that a zone principle or is it a man-to-man principle?

The editor feels that there is a place for every type of defense known to the game; that a coach should be permitted to employ any defense within the rules which he believes will enable his team to utilize best its defensive strength. So far, the National Basketball Committee has taken no steps to eliminate the use of the zone defense and, until there are certain rules limiting or restricting its usage, the zone will continue to be an important team defense used by the high school and the college coach alike.

The Three-Two was the first zone defense devised. It is given first consideration in the pages which follow. The vulnerability of the Three-Two defense to under-the-basket pressure, led to the development of the Two-

Three defense and the rebound-triangle. The Two-Three zone will be given second consideration. The defensive weakness of the Two-Three zone in the free-throw area forced the zone enthusiasts to counter by moving the center member of the rebound-triangle out to the free-throw line and this resulted in the so-called Two-One-Two zone. The Two-One-Two is possibly the most effective defensive zone to be developed and it has been placed in the third position for consideration. No attempt has been made to include attacks against the less popular zones such as the One-Two-Two, the One-Three-One, the Two-Two-One, etc.

Preparing to Meet the Zone Defense

DONALD S. WHITE

I believe that most coaches will agree that a fast-breaking offense is the best to use against any kind of a zone defense. If you can work the ball into scoring territory before your opponents have all five men stationed in their defensive positions, you have accomplished your first objective and the effectiveness of the zone has been reduced to a minimum.

However, after a basket has been made or on certain out-of-bounds plays, it is impossible to fast-break. Therefore, a well-planned set offense to be used against a set zone defense should be understood and practiced by your players.

I would like to discuss the fast break as the most important weapon to use against any type of zone. Since our primary offense is the fast break, we do not have to spend time on new fundamentals or a change in our fast-break pattern. If we know the personnel, or if we have an opportunity to scout our opponents, we try to determine the following:

1. The names, numbers and positions of players who are slow in returning to their defensive positions.
2. What defensive areas the foregoing men cover.
3. Whether the men already in position move out of their areas to cover-up for their slower teammates.

If we do not have the above information, we try to get it as soon as possible after the start of the game. Therefore, on our fast break, we try to work the ball as quickly as possible into the areas left unguarded by the opponents' slower defensive men. We also move our best set shots into these areas whenever possible.

If our fast break is able to secure this advantage, we then treat the zone as a man-to-man defense. We try to overload the protected areas in order to keep defensive men in their positions so that we will have men open for a pass if a defensive man tries to cover the areas left unguarded by their slower teammates.

We have found this method extremely helpful and if you have not tried it, do so. You will be pleased with the results.

We make very few changes in our fast break. However, our set offense is quite different and we spend much of our practice session time developing this offense.

The main principle of a zone defense is to have five men between the ball and the basket. We know that the area covered by all five men is governed by the position of the ball and that each defensive man must move quickly with the ball or certain areas will not be protected. Believing this, we place our men on certain spots in our frontcourt with the idea of spreading our opponents and compelling them to cover as much of the frontcourt as possible.

Here again it is important to know the size and ability of each defensive player. Do they shift fast with the moving ball and do they possess the endurance to do so for the entire game?

We base our set system of attack on the following principles:

1. Spreading our players.
2. Moving the ball with fast, accurate passes.
3. Placing our set shooters where they hit the best.
4. Holding up our cutting until the ball passes the front line of the defense.
5. Using the passing lanes.

By moving the ball fast from guards to forwards and "around the horn" you are able to pull the defense out of position and open up unprotected areas into which offensive men may move and then work the ball in for lay-ups, short set-shots or one-handers, and medium long shots.

Passing Lanes

against a

Zone Defense

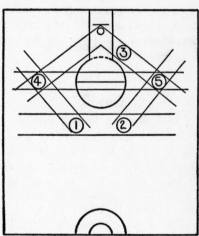

Attacking the Three-Two Zone

FORREST C. ALLEN

It should be noted in charting these penetrating offensive plays against a zone defense that the setup of the offense is identical with that used in penetrating the man-to-man defense. To be effective, both setups *must look* the same to the opponents. However, the path of the ball is very different. Furthermore, if the zone defense should drop deeper into defensive territory, the offense should pull its three-man line up to within eight or ten feet of the first line of the zone defense. This is absolutely necessary to make the offense function against this retreating defense.

Play 1

Player 4 snaps the ball to 3 and immediately cuts across in front, calling for the return pass. Just as 4 goes past 3, 3 push-passes the ball to 2, who comes straight forward from his position to receive the ball. Player 3 feints slightly to his right and then quickly cuts to the left to receive the return pass from 2. In the interim, 4 has continued over to the opposite corner of the court, apparently for the purpose of screening 1's guard. At this juncture, 1 cuts out in front of the free-throw area. Player 4, instead of

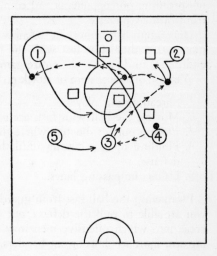

screening 1's guard, follows quickly to his own left near the side of the court. Player 3 immediately snaps the ball to 4 who is in a splendid position to shoot a side shot for the basket, preferably a carom.

Play 2

Player 4 snaps the ball to 3 and then cuts diagonally across the court calling for the return pass from 3. In reality, he is continuing on for the apparent purpose of screening 1's guard. As soon as 3's passing lane is cleared by 4, he (3) snaps the ball to 2 who comes up quickly from his position to receive the ball. Player 3 drives to an unguarded spot and receives the return pass from 2. Player 4 floats off to his own side of the court as he did in zone offense Play 1. Then, he receives a snap pass from 3, but in-

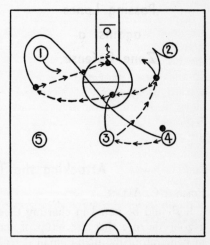

stead of shooting as he did in Play 1, he snaps the ball back to 3, who by this time has worked himself into a position for a shot.

Basic Formation

This formation surrounds the defense and uses fast passes around the outside working for side set shots, endline shots for the center (4) and front set shots for the guards (1) and (2). The attack can overload by moving one of the wing men to the opposite side and corner as shown by the movement of player 3.

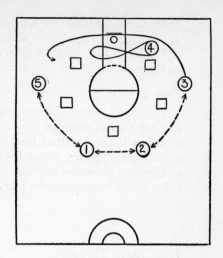

John J. Gallagher

We usually overload four men in one half of the court and place our best set shooter on the opposite side. In addition to set shooting against a zone, we like to cut between the two defensive lines and work in back of the rear line.

Basic Formation

Player 1 is the pivot man. Players 4 and 5 are good set shooters and cutters. Players 2 and 3 are our best passers and defensive men. Player 1 helps a lot, of course, if 2 and 3 are good set shots when the zone is an extremely compact one. Since the fast break is undoubtedly one of the most dangerous weapons a team using a zone defense employs, it is important that 2 and 3 protect the defensive balance of the attack.

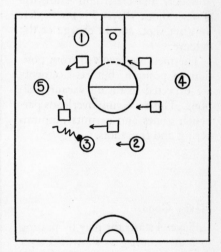

Jack Gardner

We call the attack first illustrated the Four Men Through attack. In addition to the formation, we stress the following principles in preparation for the attack:

I. *Individual technique:*

    a. Deceptive passing.

    b. Fake and dribble.

c. Set shots, medium and long are stressed.

d. No telegraphing of shots or passes.

e. Patience. Take no chances in passing or forcing a play.

f. Frequent use of the bounce pass.

II. *Team Strategy:*

a. Fast break before defense gets set.

b. Keep the ball moving.

c. When leading, control the ball and pull defense out of position.

d. Use scoring zones. Shoot from these areas.

e. Maintain defensive balance.

f. Let the defense name the play.

Four Men Through Formation

Player 1 is the best ball handler. He is the apex of the attack. Player 2 is the baseline shooter and rebounder. Players 3 and 4 are the best set shots. Player 5 is the feeder, long set shot, and in charge of the defense.

The men are revolved from position to position, but replacements are expected to fill all vacant positions. This revolving overloads particular zones and permits outnumbering and free shots.

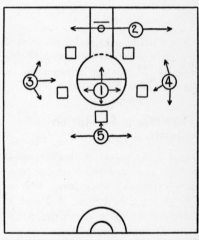

HARRY GOOD

Player 4 starts the play by passing to 2 and cutting as shown. Player 2 fakes a return pass to 4 and feeds the ball to 1 who has cut to a position on the lane. Player 3 cuts behind the rebound-guards and takes a pass from 1 under the basket.

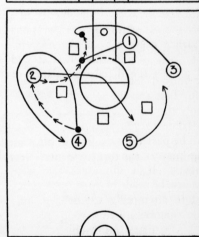

Marty Karow

Player 1 starts the play by passing to the post player (2) who breaks to the side. Player 4 breaks for the basket and the pivot player (3) breaks to the left side of the lane. Player 3 can shoot, pass to 4 or to 5. Player 5 can usually get a good corner shot.

John W. Mauer
Two-Two-One Formation

Players 1, 2, 3, 4 and 5 station themselves as indicated.

Play 1

The ball is kept moving to force the zone to slide. If the ball can be moved long enough to allow your best shooter several good set shots the zone will begin to force or come to you and then the ball can be passed inside and the attacking players can break behind the chasers. It is important that the defense be made to come out to you before attempting to use the "inside" game.

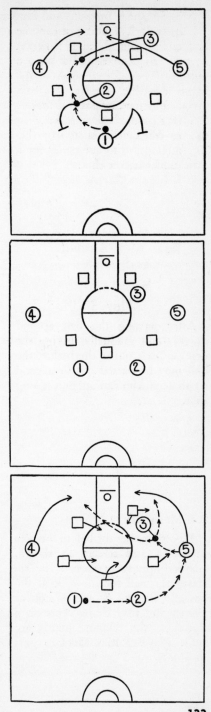

Play 2

Players 1, 2, 5 and 3 move the ball around quickly after a basket or two has been scored from the outside. Then 3 can break to the free-throw line, receive the ball, pivot and shoot, or pass off to 4 or 5 cutting for the basket. It is a *must* that several outside shots score before attempting to cut under for a close under-basket shot.

Play 3

After passing the ball around quickly and gradually driving the defense back under the basket, the ball may be passed out to a good set-shooter who can attempt a long shot.

Art McLarney

Player 1 passes the ball to the post man (5) and screens as shown. Player 5 pivots as soon as he receives the ball for the shot at the basket. Players 3 and 4 cut as shown and may change cuts on a signal so the rebound-guards are split. Player 5 may shoot or pass to 3 or 4.

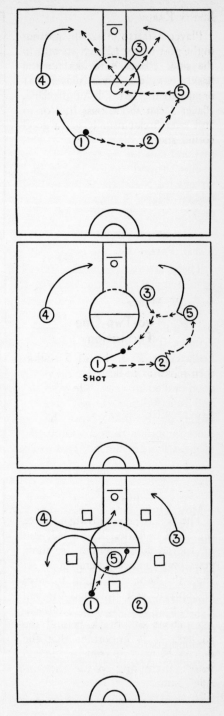

RAY S. PESCA

Player 1 starts the play by passing to 2 and screening as shown. Player 2 passes to 3 and moves slowly toward the baseline. Player 3 passes to 4 who has moved to corner. Player 4 passes back to 2 and cuts in front of the right rebound-guard. Player 2 returns ball to 4 and cuts for the basket. Player 3 cuts around under basket and screens for 5 and then cuts toward basket. Player 4 may pass to 2, 3 or 5.

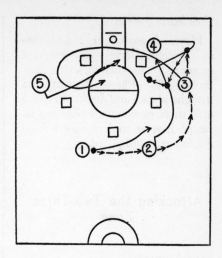

VADAL PETERSON

There are two important points to remember in planning an offense against any type of zone defense. They are: (1) Rapid ball handling. (2) A minimum of dribbling and running.

Keeping these in mind, the next thing to remember is that the proper use of a floater in the area around the basket is one way to break up a zone defense. The right kind of floater is worth his weight in gold. The wrong kind will prove to be a liability.

In picking a player for the floater assignment, look first for a man with good basketball sense. He must be able to anticipate the next defense move and function accordingly. The success or failure of the offense depends largely on this man. Next, this man must have speed and agility. This is more important than shooting ability. The other four men will have plenty of good shots at the basket if the floater plays his position properly.

Most Three-Two zones will sink the two wing chasers in to protect the center. The best way to combat this defensive setup is to play the ball to the outside with a pass from 1 to 2. As usual, the floater (5) moves from left to right. If the right rebound-guard moves back to cover 5, 3 is clear. Should the right rebound-guard elect to cover the post player (3), then 5 is free.

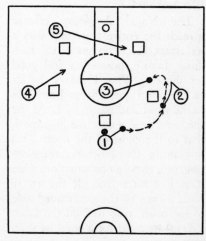

Player 1 passes to 2 and cuts straight ahead and back. Player 2 passes to 5 who cuts out to the free-throw line. Player 2 then cuts straight ahead and back. Player 5 may shoot or pass to 4 who has replaced him or to 3 cutting behind the left rebound-guard.

Attacking the Two-Three Zone

Lew Andreas

The offense lines up with 4 under the basket, and 1, 2, 3 and 5 spread in a half circle as shown. The ball is passed from 1 to 2 to 3 and finally to 4, who has moved to the corner. Player 1 fakes left and breaks for the basket and 4 feeds him a backhand pass. Player 1 has the option of shooting, stopping, pivoting, or passing off to 5. Fast ball moving and good feinting by 1 and 3 make this play a very effective one for a close shot.

Ben Carnevale

The Naval Academy offense spreads the entire zone and uses a set attack based on good ball handling, faking, possession and good set shooting. Play 1 shows the attack to the right. Player 1 dribbles to the right and passes to 3. At the the same time, 4 cuts to a pivot position to the right of the lane. This sets up a four-on-three, three-on-two, or a two-on-one situation. One man is always free. If the entire zone moves to the overloaded side of the court, pass to 2 on the other side of the court for a good set shot.

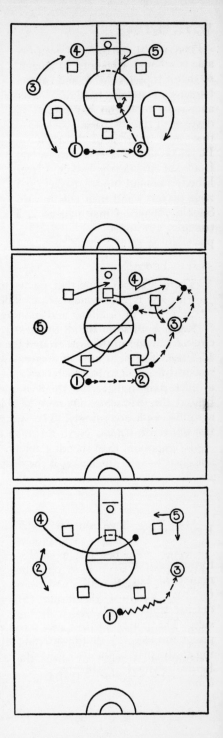

136

W. H. H. Dye

Pivot player 5 keeps breaking to side of court to which ball is passed so that a triangle may be set up between 2, 3 and 5 or between 3, 4 and 5. By means of the triangle so developed, the defensive players in that area may be outnumbered. Player on the weak side (side away from the triangle which is established) may cut behind the nearest zone players and toward the basket. Should player 1 cut in behind the triangle, a wing forward must replace him to protect the defense.

Tom Haggerty

Player 4 cuts to the free-throw circle receiving a bounce pass from 1. Player 3 cuts from behind the second line of defense and receives a quick pass from 4. Player 5 cuts behind the defensive line, receives a shuttle pass from 3, and goes in fast under the basket.

Ken Loeffler

Players 4 and 5 shuttle cross-court forming a triangle with the corner man (2). The ball is fed in from the back middle court to prevent defense from overshifting to either side. The player on the side opposite the ball (3) shuttles according to the play of the back line defensive rebounder on his side of the court.

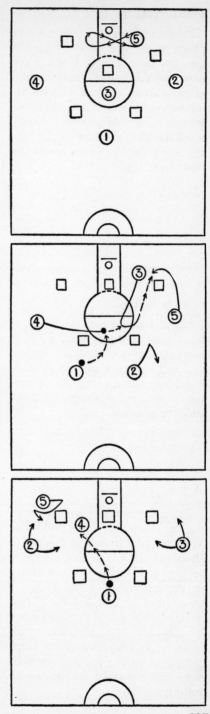

137

Vadal Peterson

Player 1 passes to 3 who quickly passes to the post player (2). On the pass from 3 to 2, 3 and 4 cut hard for the basket, while 5 maneuvers across the slot underneath the basket. Player 5 is usually free because the two outside guards cover the men breaking for the basket, while the other man covers the post player (2).

Gordon Ridings

Player 1 passes to 2 on the post. Simultaneously, players 3, 4 and 5 move as shown. A fast pass from 1 to 2 and the quick movement of 3, 4 and 5 results in a four-on-three situation with every player in a good shooting position.

Gus Tebell

Player 5 passes to 4 and covers as shown. Player 4 pivots suddenly. With the pass from 5 to 4, 1 and 2 shuttle to the left side of the court setting up a three-on-two situation in the left corner zone. Player 4 passes to 1 or 2 or shoots. Player 3 on the right side of the court fakes a cut behind the right defensive rebounder to keep him from dropping over to the left side to help out. Players 3 and 5 are responsible for the defense.

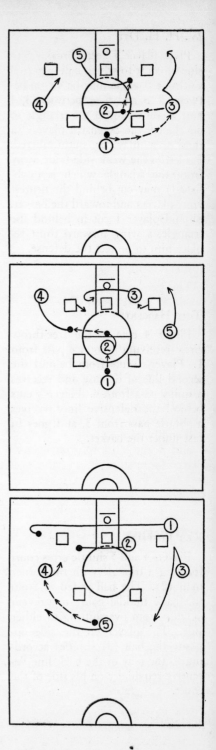

JOHN WARREN

Player 1 passes to 2 and covers the pass. Player 2 fakes toward the basket and breaks out to the ball. Player 5 breaks with the pass from 1 to 2 and sets up a pivot position on the lane. Player 3 cuts to the right of 5 and the passer (2) cuts to the left. Player 4 replaces 3 on the free-throw line.

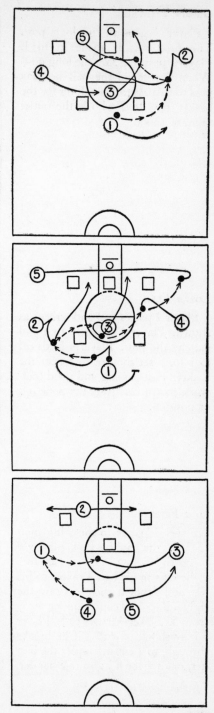

JOHN WIETHE

This play calls for fast passing but opens up several good shots because of the four-on-three situation which develops as soon as 2 receives the ball. Player 1 passes to 2. As soon as 2 receives the ball everyone moves. Player 3 steps toward the ball and receives the pass. Players 4 and 5 cut as shown. Player 3 pivots around after receiving the ball and bounce-passes to 4. Players 2 and 3 cut hard for the basket. Player 4 may shoot, pass to 2 or 3 or to 5 for a shot from the right hand corner.

Attacking Two-One-Two Zone

HARRY COMBES

Players 1 and 3 are our best shooters from the side of the court. Player 2 floats along the endline. The main objective is to get the ball to 3. If not, the ball is returned to 4 who passes to 5 who has replaced 3. If challenged by either of the guards he would pass the ball to 2 who moves to the area vacated by the challenging guard.

George Dahlberg

Player 3 goes to the long post. The first pass is made in to 1. Player 1 passes to 3 on the long post. When 3 receives the ball he may pass to 4, pass to 1 breaking for the basket, pass to 5 who is the outlet man, or shoot.

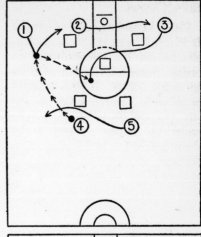

Loren Ellis

Player 2 passes to 3 and screens as shown. Player 3 passes in to 4 and cuts by the post. Player 4 feeds off to 1 for a set shot, or to 5 near the basket. Fast passing and good footwork soon maneuvers the zone out of position.

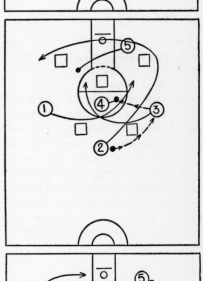

Jack Friel

Player 1 passes to the wing man (3) on the right. Post player 4 meets the ball and fakes a pass to 3 as he cuts by. Then 4 pivots to his left and fakes a shot to draw the right under-basket rebounder away from 5. Player 4 passes to 5. Player 5 may shoot, pass to 3 if he breaks through, to 2 cutting under the basket, or to 4 for a jump one-hander.

Blair Gullion

Player 1 passes to 4 after faking to 2. Player 4 meets the pass and dribbles behind 1's screen toward the basket. Sometimes he can continue on in for a score. If he is blocked, he passes to 3 who dribbles out and sets up a post. Player 4 continues on under the basket. Player 3 can shoot, pass to 1 or to 5 cutting across the lane.

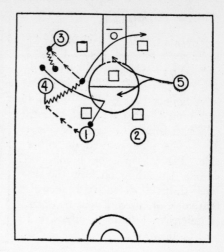

Howard Hobson

Building a sound attack against a zone defense is one of the more neglected phases of basketball today. The following suggestions are offered:

1. Improvement in set shooting beyond the 24-foot mark (necessary to supplement any zone attack).
2. Insistence on adequate and uniform facilities that will eliminate conditions that are conducive to the use of the zone—such as short or narrow courts, low ceilings, etc.
3. Use of a fast-break offense that can attack before the zone defense can get well organized and set.
4. The use of an offensive formation against the set zone that is similar to or the same as that used to attack the man-to-man defense.

Basic Formation

This is the formation used at Yale for attacking the zone and two plays with variations set up against the typical Two-One-Two zone defense. With slight changes, the same method may be used to attack other types of zones. Passing the zone out of position, using a cutter, and the use of some screens are advisable in attacking the zone.

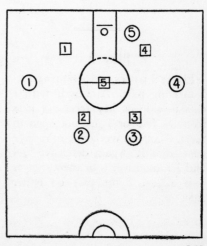

Play 1

Player 3 passes to 4 which draws defensive 4 to him. Player 4 passes to 5, who meets pass. As 3 passes to 4, 2 cuts fast into side of key to receive bounce pass from 5. Player 1 cuts under basket on weak side to take pass from 2. Player 3 is safety. The same play is used on either side. Players 5, 2 or 1 may be scorers depending on how the defense shifts. If defensive 5 takes offensive 5, offensive 2 will be open. If defensive 1 takes 2, offensive 1 will be open, etc.

Play 1A

Player 3 passes to 4 who passes to 5 meeting pass on side of key, as 2 cuts to original spot of 5. Player 1 cuts under basket on weak side. Player 5 scores or passes to 2 or 1 depending on how defense shifts. Player 3 is safety. Same play on either side.

Play 2

Player 3 passes to 4 who passes to 5 meeting pass. At this instant, 1 cuts to side of key receiving pass from 5. If 5 or 1 are not open to score, 2 cuts on weak side to receive pass from 1. Again defensive 5, 4 and 1 must cover four men. Player 3 is safety. Same play on either side.

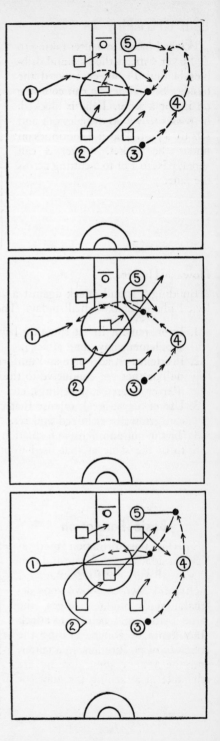

Play 2A

Player 3 passes to 4 to 5 to 1 as in original play. If there is no opening, 1 returns pass to 4 who passes to 2 who has cut from weak side to strong side corner. Player 2 will be open for short set shot.

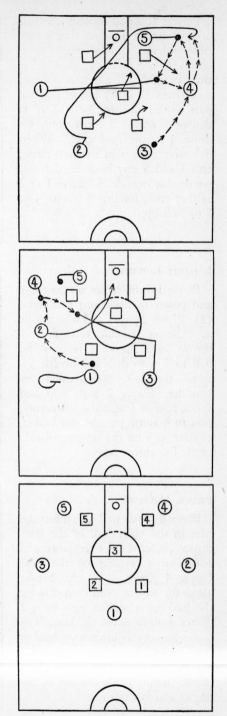

JAKE LAWLOR

Player 1 passes to 2 and follows over for protection. Player 2 passes to 4 breaking to the ball. Player 3 drives straight ahead and then cuts across and behind 2 to receive a pass on the post near the free-throw circle. Player 3 may pass to 2, 5 under the basket, or back to 4, or shoot. Player 2 must cut after passing to 4 so that the under-basket rebounders are split.

JOHN LAWTHER

Basic Formation

Editor's Note: John Lawther was undoubtedly the outstanding Two-One-Two zone coach in basketball. His Penn State teams used it exclusively with excellent results.

Players 1, 2 and 3, whip the ball around until a good set shot is possible and/or a third defensive man covers (some defensive man other than 1 and 2). If a defensive backcourt man (4 or 5) moves out, we pass to the baseline for a shot. If defensive player 3 moves out, we move 4 to the foul circle. When defensive 3 stays in the foul circle, and 4 and 5 stay back on defense, we dribble outside defensive 1 or 2 as they rush, forcing defensive 4 or 5 to pick up.

EMMETT LOWERY

Player 1 dribbles fast up the court and passes to backcourt teammate (2). Player 2 passes to 3 who breaks as close as possible toward free-throw line. Player 3 returns the ball to 2 who dribbles directly toward the left under-basket rebounder. Player 2 may stop and shoot, pass to 3 near the left corner, pass to 4 cutting under the basket, or over to 5 on the uncovered side of the free-throw lane.

FRANK McGUIRE

Player 1 passes to 2 who meets the pass in the outer half of the free-throw circle. Player 2 pivots and passes to 4 coming up the side. Player 4 passes to 5 who breaks along the baseline and then cuts for the basket. After his pass to 4, 2 drives straight down the lane. The under-basket rebounders are held in position by the cutting of 2 and 4 leaving 5 free for a good shot. This attack comprehends the use of triangles and fast passing.

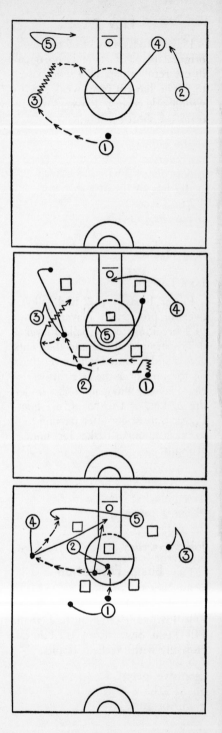

W. J. Trautwein

In attacking the Two-One-Two zone we like to work our players from a Two-Two-One position attack into a One-Three-One attack. This can be best explained by the following plays.

Play 1

Player 1 passes the ball to 2. Player 2 dribbles to the left and outside the defensive chaser on that side of the court. Player 3 breaks across to the free-throw line when 1 passes the ball to 2. Player 2 passes to 3 on the free-throw line and continues his cut as shown. Player 3 is now in the post position and we have established our One-Three-One attack. Player 3 may return-pass to 2, bounce-pass under the basket to 5 if he is unguarded, shoot himself, or pass to 4 on the unguarded side.

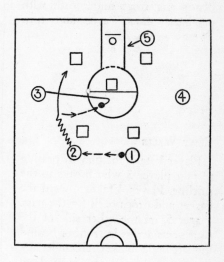

Play 2

Player 2 passes the ball to 3 and cuts to the right of defensive player 2. The movement of the ball and the cutting of 2 forces a shift in the defense. Player 3 may shoot or, if defensive 4 comes out to stop the shot, pass the ball to teammate 2. If the pass is made to 2, he will have several options all depending upon the slides made by defensive players 3, 4 and 5. Player 2 may pass to 5 under the basket if he beats defensive 5 across the lane, over to 4 cutting under from the weak side, or back to 3 or attempt a one-hand shot himself.

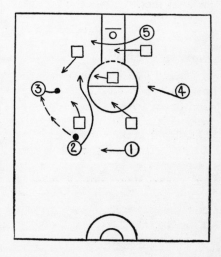

147

This formation illustrates the scoring position to which we have worked. Player 1 is our active back-court outlet player. Player 2 is our ball handler, cutter and one-hand shooter. Players 3 and 4 are our set shooters. Player 5 (our deep man) is a good tap-in player and best scorer from underneath with one-hand shots, pivot and turn shots.

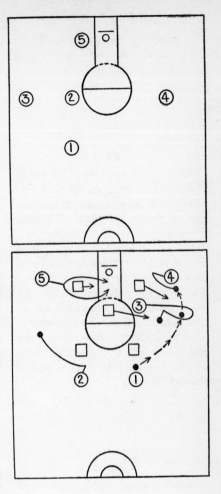

Cliff Wells

Player 1 starts the play by passing to post player 3 who breaks to the sideline. Player 4 fakes toward the basket and drops back for the pass. Player 5, on the other side of the court, cuts across in front or behind the left under-basket rebounder. By fast passing an attempt is made to secure a good shot for 3, 4 or 5. If a shot by these three is not possible, they look for 2 on the left sideline for a set shot.

Part III

THE QUICK BREAK

THE QUICK BREAK

Frank Keaney is placed in the lead-off position because his entire offense is concerned with the quick break and attending "press" tactics. The other coaches, in this chapter, supplement their quick break with a set offense.

Quick-Break Offensives

FRANK KEANEY

The fast break is used exclusively at Rhode Island State. That means we use the fast break when we have five-on-four, four-on-three, three-on-two, two-on-one, or one-on-one. The long catcher's pass is our chief weapon. This long one-handed pass must be thrown accurately from fifteen to ninety feet. To throw this pass accurately requires many hours of practice. I have never had a team with five men who were excellent one-handed passers.

All passes must be caught on the run and the receiver must be able to shoot, pivot, feint, fake, dribble, etc., while moving at full speed. This method may look like a crazy way to play (it has been called everything under the sun) but on careful analysis, it will prove to be a sane game, and with the short players who were usually available to us at Rhode Island State, the right game to play.

This pressing style calls for coverage of opponents all over the floor for the whole game. This demands superb conditioning and the ability to keep going for the full period of the game. We try to force our opponents to make mistakes by playing them all over the floor.

Whenever we make an interception, receive the ball because of a violation, etc., we start a fast break with as few passes as possible before we shoot. Of course, in this kind of a speedy game, we make a lot of misplays. However, that is to be expected because everyone knows that more speed will produce more mistakes.

Finally, we try to make the other fellow play our game. This frequently happens. And what a sorry mess a team can make out of long passes and speedy dashes up and down the court unless that team has been subjected to many hours of concentrated practice on this type of game.

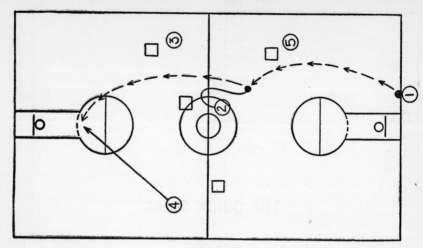

Play 1

Player 1 gets possession of the ball after a basket or outside ball. Player 2 is the best offensive player at catching, handling the ball, faking, feinting, dribbling, in team play and in brain work.

Players 3 and 4 are forwards. Players 1 and 5 are the best rebounders and the best throwers of the long pass.

In this play, 1 throws a long pass to 2 who pivots and sends a long, overhand catcher's pass to 4 who just jumps the ball into the basket. So we have a score with just two fast, long passes.

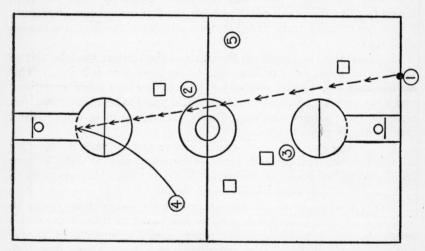

Play 2

In this case, 1 sees 4 ahead of his guard and decides to throw a long overhand catcher's pass to 4. This pass is thrown from eighty to ninety feet, just like a catcher throwing to second base. It is a fast pass and a beauty to watch but it requires considerable practice to master.

152

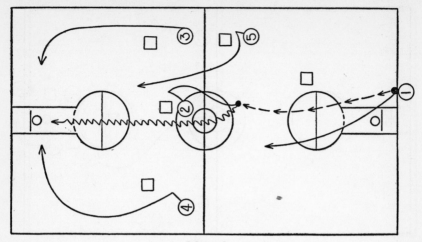

Play 3

In this situation, the defensive team has its maximum defense. Player 1 throws a long, 50-foot catcher's pass to 2. Player 2 then pivots and looks toward his basket. If either 4 or 5 have not gotten the jump on their opponent, 2 starts to fake or feint his man out of position. We will assume he gets his opponent off balance and dribbles in for the shot. Notice that 4 and 3 have broken hard down the sidelines and 1 and 5 have taken paths to the right and to the left of 2.

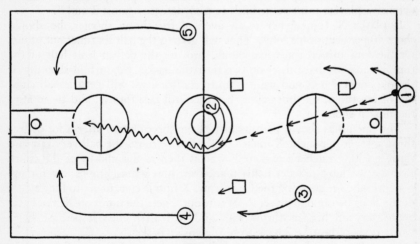

Play 4

In this play, 2 is free and this is essential for 2 is the man to have free on this fast break. We practice this play long and every day, for this is our winning play. Player 2, upon receiving the 50-foot pass, pivots and dribbles straight up the middle. Near the free-throw line the action takes place according to the moves the two defensive players nearest the basket make. The three-on-two situation wins games.

153

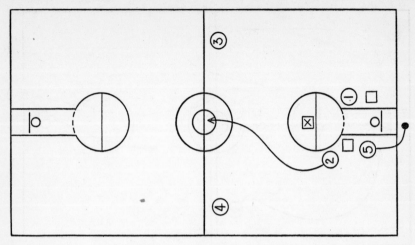

Play 5

This is a fast break after a free throw. The diagram shows our line-up when the opponents have a free throw. Player X is the free-throw shooter for the opponents. Our best rebounder is 5. Player 2 is our crafty boy, good at using his head and at all other things pertaining to basketball. Player 1 is our second best rebounder.

Notice that we play 3 and 4 near the middle of the court and toward the sidelines. This line-up compels the opponents to play your game as two defensive players must come back to play defense against 3 and 4.

If player X (opponent) is an average free-throw shooter, he should shoot 60 per cent of his fouls. That will give us the ball six times out of ten. Of the four missed shots, we should procure the ball at least half of the time because we have three-on-two near the basket. So, in foul shooting, if the opponent shoots and we live up to statistics, we will get the ball eight out of ten times, six times after the successful free throws, and twice after the missed shots.

The line-up as shown permits us to have three-on-two after a lot of free throws, for it opponent X makes the foul, 5 retrieves the ball very fast and throws a long catcher's pass to 2, who is then at the middle of the court. Because we have practiced this maneuver, it is almost impossible for opponents who are shooting the free throw, X in this case, to get to the middle of the floor before our player 2. When our 2 gets the jump on X, the latter gets jittery on his free-throw shot and will often miss it because he is worried about beating 2 back to his defensive basket.

Naturally, when 5 retrieves the ball and throws up court to 2 by means of a long, baseball pass, we have the old familiar situation of three-on-two and then it is up to player 2 to prove that he is capable of taking advantage of the opportunity by scoring or passing to a teammate for a two-pointer.

If player 2 has a clear lane to the goal he should continue to drive under the basket. If he cannot see daylight he should stop at the free-throw line and pass to a teammate or shoot from that position.

154

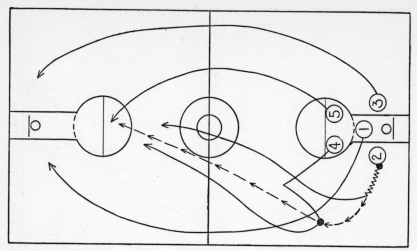

John Bunn

Play 1

Player 5 breaks hard for his basket as soon as he sees 1, 2 and 3 are in good rebound position. Player 4 starts with 5. Assuming 2 gets the rebound, as soon as he starts his dribble away from the basket, 3 and 1 break for their basket. Player 4 reverses to meet the pass from 2, and then passes ahead to 5. All players follow the paths shown up court.

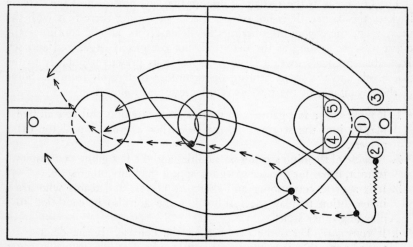

Play 2

Player 5 breaks as in Play 6. Player 4 breaks up court. Player 2 starts his dribble and 1 and 3 start up court hard. Player 4 pivots back to meet the pass from 2. Player 2 passes to 4 and drives up the center of the court. Player 5 stops up court, breaks back to meet 4's pass, and then passes forward to 3.

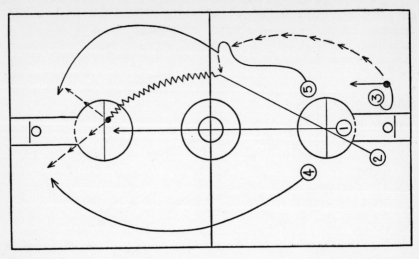

Everett Dean

Player 3 recovers ball from backboard and passes to 5 on the right sideline. Player 5 passes to 2 near midcourt. Player 2 dribbles to the free-throw circle and passes to the open player, (4 or 5). Naturally, if player 2 is not covered, he will attempt the score himself.

Howard Hobson

The fast break is the system of offense that attempts to beat the defense back to the basket. It is not only a matter of getting there first with the most men, thereby outnumbering the defense, but also it continues the effort to score so long as the defense is not completely organized and set. Basketball probably owes a large measure of its present popularity to the fast break and the many scoring opportunities that result from it. Some of the advantages of the fast break offense are as follows:

1. It makes for a fast game with more scoring attempts and gets all five players into the scoring. It, therefore, has a great appeal for the players.
2. Because of the high scoring possibilities and the fast game that results from it, it has far greater spectator appeal than any other style.
3. It is a great conditioner and therefore players and teams who are in condition to play the fast-break game are also in condition to play any other style.
4. It constantly keeps the pressure on the defense. If the defensive team knows that the other team only employs set play tactics, it can concentrate on offensive rebounding and get back on defense slowly. The fast break is another offensive threat for the defense to worry about.

Following, are two typical fast-break plays. Many options and variations are possible. Right here, it might be wise to insert a word of caution to

156

the coach who plans to use the fast break. A good fast break should definitely not be considered a hit or miss, slam-bang slap-stick style of basketball. Fast-break plays must be as well organized as any other type of play. They must have organization that gives each player a definite assignment and they must have rebound organization and defensive organization to be sound. A few points to remember in executing the fast break are as follows:

1. The first pass out is all important. Go to meet passes and the passer should be sure the receiver is open—take no chances on interceptions.
2. Dribble only when no one is open ahead—then dribble for the basket.
3. Those breaking ahead should run hard to the end of the court then break out to meet the ball. This carries the defense to the end of the court and opens plays.
4. Do not dribble or pass into corners on the break as a general rule.
5. Your backboard assignment is a definite part of the play—and means baskets.
6. Make only passes that advance the ball—not cross-court. Men cutting should make sharp cuts—not run in circles.
7. When you have two-on-one, dribble for the basket and force the defense to commit himself. Shoot at your first opportunity while you have defense outnumbered.

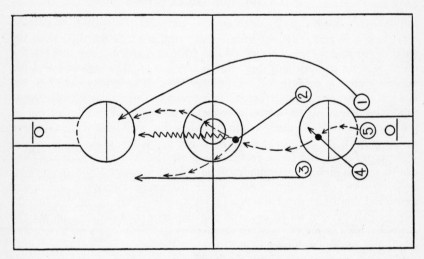

Play 1

Player 5 retrieves the rebound and passes to 4 who cuts cross-court into key. Player 4 passes to 2 who cuts into center area of court. Player 2 passes to 3 or 1 whichever is open or he may dribble down center to create a three-on-two situation. Player 4 trails and rebounds at the end of the break. Player 5 is the safety.

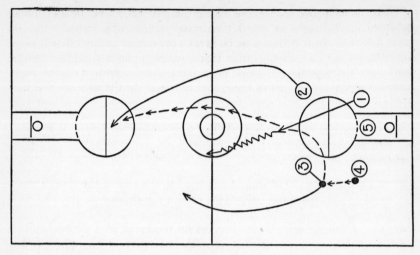

Play 2

Player 4 retrieves the rebound and passes to 3 who meets the pass on the side of the court. Player 3 passes ahead to 1 driving for midcourt. Player 1 may dribble or pass ahead to 2. Player 4 trails and rebounds at the end of the break. Player 5 is the safety.

Drills for the Quick Break

Herbert W. Read

I think it is generally recognized that a quick break usually comes off an interception, the recovery of a loose ball, or a sharp rebound. Then a quick peg out is made and the "run" is on its way. The pass out may get entirely over the defense for a simple drive-in shot; it may put three attackers against one defender, two against one, or three against two. Sometimes the defending team may even be all back but off balance or out of position, and the drive can go right through. The swiftness of the offensive action permits no diagnosis; so speed is the prime essential.

Patterns for a quick-break movement down the floor are common. They can be seen in almost any publication on basketball. A pass out to a button-hooking forward, a simple weave where the opposite forward and center cross, and the three man fan-out is on its way—the man in the middle taking the ball straight down the center of the floor on a dribble, forcing the defensive man or men to commit themselves and then a pass off to flankers coming in under the basket.

However, there is something else besides these patterns that gets a quick break going well. Basketball is definitely a habit game. Fast break habits of ball handling, the strong emphasis being on wrist and finger action rather than on the slower full arm motion; elimination of any movement in drills that would tend to slow up the play; forgetting the principles of protecting the ball with the body but rather keeping it away from the defense by getting rid of it—these all play a part in the fast action needed for a good break.

Then, there is such a thing as setting the pace of the action. There are modified quick breaks in which the defensive man who recovers the ball takes a look to see if he has a quick-break opportunity. But this will never have the speed of an all-out quick break, based on the assumption you always have the opportunity and then making the decision. You can make mistakes in this type of quick break and now and then your team will look pretty bad—on their flatfooted days. But when it works well it will have the flash that pleases the crowd.

Here is a series of drills that you can give your team which, while they will not always score according to the pattern, they will set the pace for a coordinated fast movement.

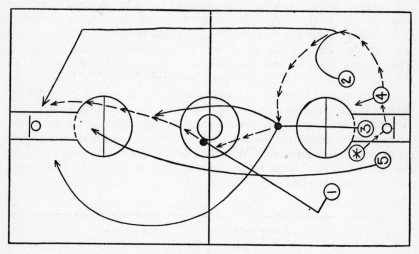

Drill No. 1

(In the preceding and in all subsequent drills, 1 will be left forward, 2 right forward, 3 center, 4 right guard, and 5 left guard.)

The Coach shoots a ball against the backboard. It is taken off by 4 who whirls in the air and gets the ball out to 2. The latter passes in to 3, then breaks straight down the sideline and cuts in to the basket. Player 1 passes to 2 who scores. Player 5 trails the play.

Run the sequences as follows:

    Play Number 1 Right: 4-2-3-1-2
    Play Number 2 Right: 4-2-3-1-2-3
    Play Number 3 Right: 4-2-3-1-2-3-5

Note that the sequences are reached by adding a pass. Hold 5 back. On his sequence, he should not be entering the foul circle until 3 has the ball on a pass from 2. The same sequences can be worked from the left side:

    Play Number 1 Left: 5-1-3-2-1
    Play Number 2 Left: 5-1-3-2-1-3
    Play Number 3 Left: 5-1-3-2-1-3-4

159

Again, note that the prime purpose of the foregoing sequence is pace setting. Passes are "spot" and exact. The speed will naturally be there but like all other patterns, modifications must be made through scrimmages.

The foregoing drill involves a recovery off the bank—that is, from a definite spot. But what to do about getting a concerted movement down the floor when the ball is recovered just anywhere; say, from a loose ball or an interception?

Part of the speed and coordination in the subsequent movement will come from being alert and fast-break minded, but some sort of orderly pattern can be worked out with an idea I developed a few years ago. I call it a "Strong Side—Weak Side Attack."

It operates as follows: When it is perceived that a ball is about to become loose the two or three men nearest break toward the area, as outfielders in baseball rush for flies that may be going into marginal territory. There is an absolute commitment of all until it is apparent who can best get it. Then, one of the other men breaks to a point one-third of the way down the nearest sideline and the other goes two-thirds down. The ball goes out to the first man and down to the second man who goes in for a score if the defense is beaten. This is the strong side operation. A fourth man goes to a mid-floor position on the opposite sideline. This establishes a weak side. From there he drives into the foul circle to take a pass if the second receiver on the strong side gets stuck. When the defense plays the strong side, then the pass out is to the weak side. The initial ball handler and the fifth man follow or trail the play.

STRONG SIDE

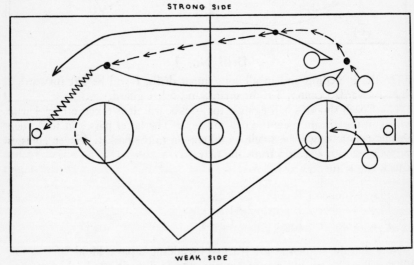

WEAK SIDE

Drill No. 2

I have spoken of the need of being very quick and alert. The two terms are not synonymous, for alertness indicates the mental state which prepares the body to move quickly.

This brings up a third pattern for floor play. I call it the "Offensive—Defensive Break" drill. Here we can restate two very old definitions which are principles for sound basketball action. *Offensive Break:* One moment before you regain the ball you should see that you are going to regain it and be ready to go on offense. *Defensive Break:* One moment before you lose the ball you should see that you are going to lose it and be ready to go on defense. But, in neither case should you fail to complete your offensive or defensive action.

The drill is set up as follows: Two teams are placed in opposite ends of the court in the positions shown. Neither has the ball. It is in the hands of the coach who stands at the center sideline.

Now both teams must be on their toes—they do not know whether they will attack or defend in the next moment.

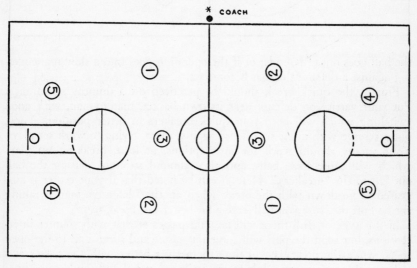

Drill No. 3

The coach makes his throw as deceptive as possible. If the ball goes to anyone on either of the front lines, this player instantly drives in with a quick-break attempt. This will be easier if the drive is done on the angles shown in the following Drill.

Drill No. 4

The ball may go to anyone on the back lines also. Then, the front offensive line drives ahead to take positions in a set offense. The back line men bring the ball up fast for a pass in to get a quick score.

It all adds up to a series of very brief scrimmages, lasting from three to about twenty seconds. The coach whistles to stop the play if a score is made on the first break; if the defensive team gets the ball on a rebound or interception and scores on a counter fast break; if there is a foul or violation; if

161

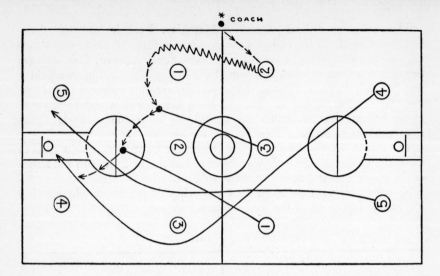

the ball goes out of bounds; or if the operation goes into a slow maneuvering against a defense that has become set.

Finally, the quick break should be practiced off a dummy scrimmage. Put your varsity on defense near its own basket, man-to-man, with good switching which will keep your quick breakers in better position. Then, put a reserve with a fair set offense against them, trying to work set plays. Your varsity should work for interceptions, at least, breaking up plays which will cause loose balls, and also rebound strongly, getting the ball out fast to the "breakers." Here, it can be noted that if your center is also geared to go down with the break when another defensive man is taking the ball off the bank you will have a far better fast-break team.

In this type of drill there will be wild passes at first with counter interceptions, but soon the pass will come out faster and surer, and to the open spots, while the breakers will time themselves better with the passes and will handle them better while traveling at top speed and while sometimes a bit off balance. After that, it is a matter of beating whatever defenses are formed against them. Work the dummy scrimmage from both ends of the court to save time. Of course, the floor must be absolutely clear for this type of work.

162

Part IV

JUMP BALL PLAYS

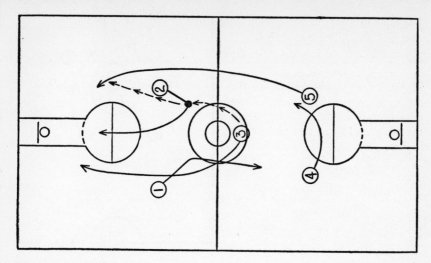

KEN GERARD

Center (3) tips the ball to forward 2, who comes in high for the tap. Guard 5 breaks down side and receives an over-the-shoulder pass or tap from 2. Player 1 breaks in toward the center and screens for 3 who breaks around and outside the screen. Player 2 follows the pass and breaks down the middle.

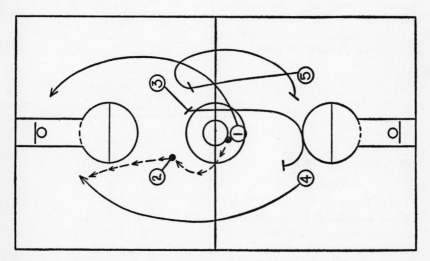

ELMER LAMPE

Center 1 taps the ball to 2 breaking in high for the tap. Player 2 bats the ball over his head to 4 breaking down on the left side of the court. Player 4 may dribble on in for a score or pass to 1 who has been double-screened by 3 and 5. Players 3 and 5 are responsible for the defense.

JOE NILAND

Player 1 taps the ball to 2 standing in the lane but outside the broken line denoting the circle. Player 2 fakes right and waits for 3 to cut behind 5's screen. After passing to 3, 2 cuts to his right and the jumper (1) cuts straight for the basket.

ELMER RIPLEY

Play 1

Player 3 taps the ball to the side. Player 5 screens for 4 who goes around to take the tap. Player 4 can either dribble to basket for a lay-up or take a short set shot.

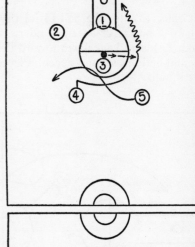

Play 2

Player 2 taps the ball to 3. Player 3 tosses or taps the ball with both hands directly over his head and far down the middle of the court. Players 4 and 5 fake forward and then cut down court at full speed.

Part V

OUT-OF-BOUNDS PLAYS

Play 1

Player 1, out of bounds, passes to 2, 3 or 4. Note the screening.

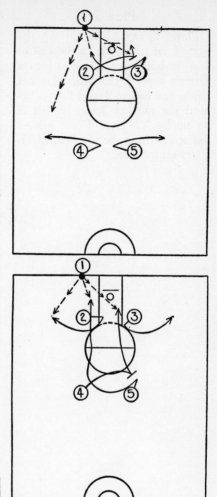

Play 2

Player 1, out of bounds, passes to 2, 4 or 5. Note the screening.

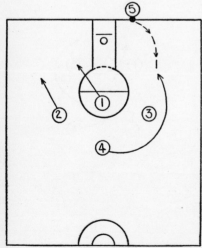

AL BAGGETT

Play 1

Player 5, out of bounds, passes to 4 cutting around 3. Players 1 and 2 cut to the opposite side. Player 3 can back up for a safety pass after teammate 4 cuts past his screen.

Play 2

Player 5, out of bounds on the side of the court, passes the ball to 4 in the backcourt. Player 1 breaks directly toward the ball. Player 4 passes the ball to 1 and breaks behind the moving screen which is set up by 2. Player 5 cuts behind the screen near the sideline which 3 sets up for him.

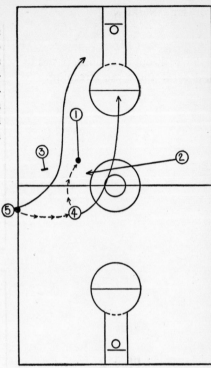

Al Duer

Play 1

Player 5, out of bounds, may pass to teammate breaking free. Player 1 screens across lane for 2. Player 4 uses touch-and-go screen to free teammate 3.

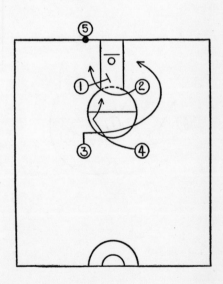

Play 2

Player 5, out of bounds, can get a quick pass to 1 or 2 here for a quick shot. Player 4 again uses a touch-and-go screen to free teammate 3.

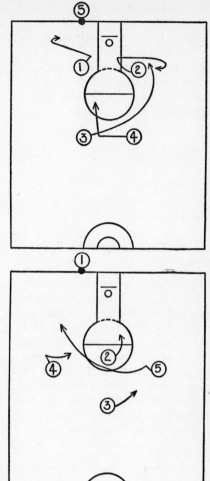

FRED ENKE

Play 1

Player 1, out of bounds, may pass to the player breaking free. Player 5 breaks around the facing block set up by 2 on the free-throw line. Players 3 and 4 drive in to the right. Player 3 is safety receiver.

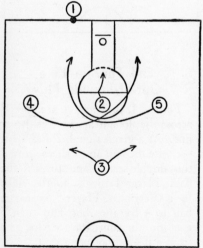

Play 2

Player 1 hits the teammate working free. Players 4 and 5 split the facing post (2). After they pass, 2 cuts straight down the lane. Player 3 is again the safety receiver.

Player 1, out of bounds, passes to 2 who signals for 3 to screen for him. If the opponents switch, 1 passes to 3. Player 1 follows his pass. Players 4 and 5 cross in the backcourt for an outlet pass.

NAT HOLMAN

Side Out-of-Bounds Play

This play has been used successfully by City College for a number of years. Player 1 throws the ball to 3 and drives in hoping to trap his guard into his teammate, 2. If 1 gets clear, 3 whips a pass down the middle of the floor to 1 as he goes up for the shot. If 1 should be trapped and stopped at this particular moment, 4 drives in behind 5's screen. Player 1 can spin then, and feed the ball to 4 for a shot.

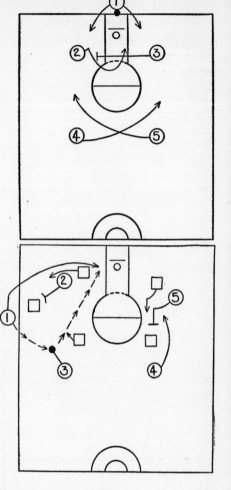

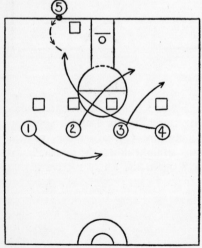

End Four in Line Out-of-Bounds Play

Players 1, 2, 3 and 4 are spread across the floor near the free-throw line. At a given signal, 2 and 3 cut opposite the ball and 4 slices around this double-screen and toward the ball. Player 1 breaks to the right for a safety pass. Player 5 passes the ball to 4 for the shot, and then 5 cuts into the court for a return pass from 4 if 4 cannot get a shot.

End Four in Circle Out-of-Bounds Play

Players 1, 2, 3 and 4 are spread across the court beyond the free-throw circle in a circle. Player 5 passes the ball to 2 who fakes left and cuts laterally to the right. At the same time, 4 screen-blocks teammate 3's opponent and 3 drives into the basket. Player 2 passes to 3 cutting under the basket for the shot. Note that 5, after passing the ball to 2, comes into the court and screen-blocks teammate 1's opponent so that the lane will be kept clear for the pass from 2 to 3. Player 2 can pass to 1 if 3 is not successful in freeing himself from his guard.

EUGENE LAMBERT

Players 3 and 5 cut toward the ball out of bounds in 1's hands. Player 4 retreats for a safety pass. Player 2 cuts through the hole his teammate 4 leaves in the line and behind 5.

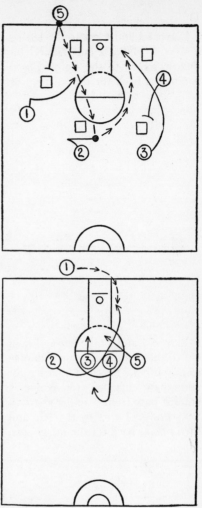

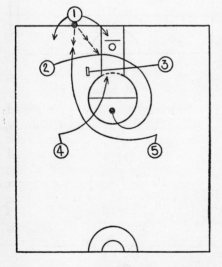

AL MCCLELLAN

On a given signal, players 2, 3 and 5 move simultaneously. Player 4 waits until the screens are in the right position and then cuts directly down the lane. Player 2 circles and assumes a position back of the free-throw line for the safety pass. Best receivers are 4 and 5 but the pass may be made to 3 standing on the lane. Player 1 follows his pass.

Donald Moore

Players 3 and 4 cut to the left on a signal. Player 2 cuts behind the double screen to the right. Player 5 remains back for the safety pass.

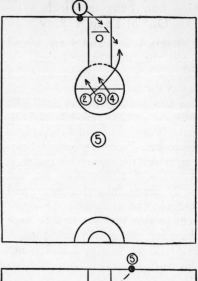

Nibs Price

Players 1 and 2 fake left and then cut to the right setting up a double screen for 3. Player 3 fakes right and then cuts left to receive a bounce pass from 5 under the basket. Player 4 cuts to the left and then breaks back for the safety pass.

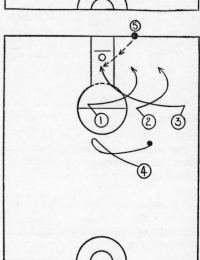

INDEX